FRUGAL LAS VEGAS
Las Vegas Guide Series
2017 Edition, Volume 1

ISBN – 13: 978-1539538370
ISBN – 10: 1539538370

Please direct any corrections, suggestions, comments, questions, or requests to: frugallasvegas@yahoo.com
Updated July 2017

DISCLAIMER:

The travel/hotel/restaurant/gaming industries, especially in Las Vegas, are extremely volatile. Businesses close and re-open. Casino resorts are built, acquired and sold. Policies, rates, hours and promotions constantly change and evolve.

Published annually, travel guides typically generalize data or avoid specific rate quotes so as not to become outdated upon publication. The date that factual representations and statements were updated and verified in this copy appears at the bottom of the copyright page.

The author has received no consideration from the businesses mentioned herein. This guide is for informational purposes only. There are no express or implied warranties as to accuracy or for the use of this information. All rates, hours, amenities, promotions, terms and conditions are subject to change. You also understand and accept responsibility for your own actions, thus releasing the author, publisher, distributors and vendors of this guide from any and all liability.

Enjoy yourself while visiting Las Vegas! Should you choose to gamble, please gamble responsibly.

TABLE OF CONTENTS

♠♥♣♦

LAS VEGAS TIPS

• Create an email account for the impending deluge of advertising emails. Use this new account for Las Vegas travel related correspondence and sign-ups. This will make it easier and quicker to locate travel related correspondence, and your regular email inbox will not be inundated with advertisements and offers.

• Sign-up for Players Clubs at the casinos you plan to patronize. Provide the aforementioned email address.

• If at all possible, avoid planning your visit during conventions or holiday periods and plan your stay midweek. Hotel rates are lowest Sunday through Thursday nights.

• Take in the sights, ambiance and amenities the "Strip" has to offer, but quality lodging can also be found off-Strip and is typically more reasonably priced.

• Utilize free and/or public transportation.

• Take advantage of casino and restaurant promotions.

• Use 50% off and Buy-One Get-One Free coupons (notated as B1G1 throughout this guide).

• Enjoy the ambiance and amenities the "Strip" has to offer, but if you gamble, better odds are offered Downtown and at off-Strip properties. If you choose to gamble, take advantage of casino Free Slot Play and Match Play offers.

• Remember that many professions in Vegas earn minimum wage and depend on tip income, but tips can add up fast. Tip fairly but not extravagantly, no more than you would at home and dependent on service. On average tip restaurant waitstaff and spa attendants 15-20%. Tip cocktail servers, buffet waitstaff, housekeepers and bell attendants $1-$2 per drink, person, day or bag. Tip dealers the amount of your bet once or twice an hour, taxi drivers 15-20% and valet attendants from $2-$5.

♠♥♣♦

FRUGALITY

♠♥♣♦

Considering you are viewing this guide, you apparently are contemplating joining the throngs of over 42 million annual visitors to Las Vegas, or are a valley resident. Regardless of your specific situation, by perusing this guide you desire to obtain the greatest value from your travel and entertainment dollars.

A valuable resource, this guide empowers you with indispensable knowledge concerning the Las Vegas valley, specifically how to stretch your budget while here. Without sacrificing lavishness, extravagance, decadence, or indulgence (that one comes to expect when in fabulous Las Vegas), this guide shows how to save hundreds of your hard earned dollars through frugality.

Frugality is defined as the quality of being frugal, sparing, thrifty, prudent and economical in the use of consumable resources such as money. Once empowered with the knowledge herein and by acquiring goods and services in a restrained manner, everyone can reap the benefits of a low cost vacation experience or night out through frugality. This guide will show that you don't need to be a high roller to get free or half-priced hotel rooms, meals, drinks, show tickets, attraction passes, helicopter tours, day trips and more! Whatever your desire, almost everything in Las Vegas is within your budget through frugality!

Las Vegas has the ability to make ordinary people feel special by catering to their self-indulgence. In the 1950s casinos made their money off gamblers. Good customers were rewarded with free rooms, food, drinks, shows and other amenities. Bad customers may have received an unwanted excursion into the desert!

On Thanksgiving 1966 businessman Howard Hughes arrived in Las Vegas and rented the Penthouse and top floor of the Desert Inn Hotel and Casino. In December, to make way for high rollers expected to arrive for New Year's Eve in the luxury suites they were occupying, Hughes and his entourage were asked to leave. Hughes refused, entering into negotiations to buy the hotel instead. In March 1967 Hughes closed the deal for $13.2 million in cash and loans and never left his room or the hotel until Thanksgiving Eve of 1970!

With the commencement of Howard Hughes' casino empire the Nevada legislature passed the *Corporate Gaming Act*, paving the way for corporations to bypass the financial background checks required to own casinos. By the mid-1970s the Nevada Gaming Control Board also began to clamp down on granting licenses to known mobsters, who were mostly eradicated from the industry by the early 1980s.

Through corporate investment and a construction boom, Las Vegas has become a sightseeing destination, fine dining mecca and entertainment venue, where casinos profit less from gaming and increasingly more from lodging, food, beverage, entertainment, retail, amenities and fees.

Unlike the Vegas of the distant past, you no longer worry about that ride into the desert, or need to purchase a hotel to get what you desire! Now every customer is made to feel special and rewarded, regardless of the size of their budget, gambler or not!

♠♥♣♦

The Las Vegas Convention and Visitors Authority's annual *Visitor Profile Study* of 2015 indicates that the average party of visitors consisted of 2.2 adults, whom stayed an average of 3.4 nights. During this stay, in addition to lodging ($116 ± per night) an average of $292 was spent on food & beverage, $61.95 on shows, $14.86 sightseeing, $122.66 shopping and $73.45 for local transportation. **www.lvcva.com**

Assuming two people are traveling together and were to budget these amounts for their own visit to Las Vegas, by acquiring goods and services in an informed and restrained manner, the savings for the stay outlined above could easily be over 50 percent! This result would be attained through the use of coupons, gift certificates, rewards, promotions, Players Club benefits and complimentaries (comps).

The best advice for those not accustomed to using coupons or other discount options, is don't be shy or embarrassed about taking advantage of the plethora of opportunities available in Las Vegas! There is no stigma attached to the use of coupons or seeking discounts. In fact, it is normal and expected behavior. Coupons, promotions and discounts are marketing tools utilized by almost every Las Vegas casino, hotel, restaurant and show venue!

♠♥♣♦

Ask yourself, when you fly do you typically pay full fare or seek a discount? Unless there is no other option available, I would guess that most people do not choose to pay full fare. Other travelers on the plane, in a seat exactly the same as yours, will arrive at the destination the same time you do, but at what price point was their seat purchased? It could have been at full retail, one of countless discount levels, a reward ticket, a companion ticket, or even a non-revenue pass. At which price point did you travel and what price would you have preferred to pay?

Just think of a Las Vegas business as an airplane. The couple sitting at another table in a restaurant for example, is enjoying the same $20 Prime Rib dinner that you and your significant other are, but at what price point? If the other couple is paying full retail, the cost would be $40 plus tax and tip. Wouldn't you prefer to enjoy the same meal at a discount of 10 to 50% off, utilize a B1G1 coupon, or perhaps even as a complimentary? Who among us would not prefer that free meal, drink, show, hotel room, shuttle ride, helicopter flight, round of golf, day trip, gift, gaming credit, or to receive cash back!

♠♥♣♦

The information at your fingertips has been personally researched and utilized over the past quarter century! As a father of five living in Las Vegas for decades, frugality was never an option, it was a necessity! It is impossible to enumerate the countless meals my family consumed and consumes in Vegas restaurants and buffets at a fraction of the cost or free!

My knowledge of hotel operations came from years at the front desk and in reservations at a small eastern resort. As a tourist I've stayed at over thirty Las Vegas valley casino/hotels! Some hotels, like Key Largo and Town Hall, have been demolished leaving vacant lots. The Aladdin, Boardwalk, Dunes, Hacienda, Stardust and Sands have been imploded and replaced. The Continental, Fitzgerald's, Imperial Palace, Maxim, Reserve, San Remo, Terrible's and Quad have been acquired, remodeled and rebranded. Bally's, Boulder Station, California, Eastside Cannery, Excalibur, Flamingo, Fremont, Gold Coast, Golden Gate, Harrah's, Luxor, Main Street Station, Monte Carlo, Orleans, Palace Station, Plaza, Red Rock Resort, Rio, Silver Sevens, Sunset Station and Wild Wild West round out my patronized hotels list!

As a consumer, my personal philosophy is to avoid hotels with a resort fee, unless I am staying on a complimentary with the fee waived (not all Vegas hotels waive the resort fee on a comp); staying on a B1G1 offer (where the resort fee is waived free nights); or when using a coupon/reward for a free night with payment of the resort fee.

Unlike the typical tourist, due to the duration of my Vegas visits, frequent hotel changes are required. In December 2015 for example, my Vegas visit was eighteen hotel nights at seven separate properties. Changing properties is not as bad as it may initially sound, especially when the price is right! Eight nights were comps (resort fees waived), six nights were B1G1 (resort fees waived on free nights) and four nights were on a promotional rate at a property with no resort fees. My total hotel cost was just $303 plus tax!

Hotel savings can be even greater when a stay straddles two contiguous months, especially once you start receiving casino marketing offers. In June/July 2016 for example, my Vegas visit was for fifteen hotel nights at six separate properties. Twelve nights were comps (resort fees waived), two nights were free on a reward (required payment of resort fees) and one night was a promotional rate at a property with no resort fees. My total hotel cost was a mere $95 plus tax! Better still, in November/December 2016 nineteen hotel nights also came in at under $100!

My knowledge of casino operations comes from working in the Slot Departments of two major casinos, from entry level to Slot Shift Manager. I've also worked on the production line at International Game Technology (IGT) refurbishing and assembling Slot & Video Poker machines. As a consumer I have experienced one form of gambling or another in three countries and four states. Years ago, and for a period of four years, I earned a living playing low limit Video Poker machines!

These are my credentials, acquired over three decades, which qualify me to give advice on saving money in Las Vegas. However, the Vegas market is extremely time sensitive. Promotions come and go. Rates, fares and fees change. Businesses open, close and are acquired. Phone numbers, emails and management change, as do policies and procedures. Therefore, once you've absorbed the information contained within this resource, it would be prudent to utilize the provided contact information to confirm the most recent data specific to your personal preferences and travel plans.

♠♥♣♦

Overwhelmed by endless hours searching the internet planning a Vegas vacation? Disheartened by the plethora of outdated information? Yes, regardless of what some websites indicate, the Las Vegas Trolley, Elvis Presley Museum, Liberace Experience, Masquerade in the Sky, Sirens of TI, Stratosphere High Roller, Polaroid Fotobar, Jeff Koons' *Tulips* sculpture, the *Lucky Cat* at the Cosmopolitan, among other attractions, have closed! An indispensible resource for the resident and visitor, this guide is packed with current information to simplify your search, and in the process, save a great deal of money in fabulous Las Vegas!

♠♥♣♦

WELCOME TO LAS VEGAS

♠♥♣♦

No visit to the extravaganza known as Las Vegas would be complete without a grand welcome from the iconic "Welcome to Fabulous Las Vegas, Nevada" sign (pictured on the cover pre-2008), which stands alone in the median of Las Vegas Boulevard (the Strip) just south of the Mandalay Bay Hotel and Russell Road.

Never trademarked, the signs iconic image was designed as a gift to the city by Betty Willis when she worked for Western Neon Company, and was installed in 1959. Technically, the welcome sign; McCarran International Airport; the University of Nevada Las Vegas and most of the Las Vegas Strip; are not in Las Vegas but in the unincorporated town of Paradise, Nevada! The Stratosphere is the only "Strip" casino hotel actually located in Las Vegas!

For decades the welcome sign was the first sign travelers encountered as they entered Vegas, a refreshing sight after hours driving through the desert! But the sign became hazardous for those choosing to stop for a photograph. Cars parked on the side of the road or in traffic lanes. People stood in the street to take a picture or jaywalked, dodging heavy traffic, making pedestrian safety an issue for decades. Since 2008 all that changed with official public access.

In 2009 the iconic sign was proposed and approved for inclusion in the *US National Register of Historic Places.* Improved and expanded in 2015, the sign (now solar powered) is a "Strip" destination with 24 hour access, serviced by two city bus routes, featuring traffic signals, marked crosswalks, a 33-car parking lot and room for tour buses.

♠♥♣♦

Las Vegas is located in Clark County, the nation's thirteenth largest county comprising 8,061 square miles. The county boasts a population over two million, mainly concentrated in the Las Vegas valley, a 600 square mile basin shaped by nature like a bowl, sloped on a downward angle from the northwest toward the southeast.

The Las Vegas valley is surrounded by mountain ranges. Looking north from the center of town, to the north/northwest, one will see the Sheep Range. More due north is the Las Vegas Range. To the east is Sunrise and Frenchman Mountains, divided by a pass. Further south and east of Frenchman, overlooking Lake Mead, are the River Mountains. Southeast of the basin in Henderson one sees the North McCullough Range. Further away and due south from the basin, lies the South McCullough Range. Looking west from the basin, beginning in the southwest to the northwest, are Mt. Potosi, Blue Diamond Hill, the Red Rock Range (Mt. Wilson, Rainbow Mtn. and Bridge Mtn.), the Summerlin Peaks, the La Madre Range and Spring Mountains (Harris Peak, Mt. Charleston and Mummy Mountain).

Nearby Mount Charleston, officially Charleston Peak, the regions highest peak at 11,918 feet (3,633 meters), is located in the Spring Mountains National Recreation Area, a year-round getaway for valley residents and visitors. Roughly a forty minute drive from Las Vegas, the mountain can be seen when looking toward the northwest. Snow-capped more than half the year, Mount Charleston offers a modest ski area, a good number of hiking trails, picnic areas and camp sites, some of which are RV accessible.
 www.gomtcharleston.com

If this will be your first visit to Las Vegas, you may be interested in viewing an excellent full color brochure published by the Las Vegas Convention Authority. **www.lasvegas.com/planning-tools/free-visitors-guide**

♠♥♣♦

In the Vegas valley, when tourists are added to the traffic mix, rush hour, weekend and event traffic can become a living nightmare. Even so, Vegas is easy to get around with streets laid out on an east/west and north/south grid system. Interstate 15 (north/south) runs parallel to Las

Vegas Boulevard which divides east from west for most major streets. Charleston Boulevard divides north from south. (Be aware that a few streets will run into each other and change names.)

The 4.5 mile section of Las Vegas Boulevard South, which extends from Russell Road to Sahara Avenue, is better known as the "Strip." The Strip is situated within what is known as the "Strip Corridor," which runs from Valley View Boulevard on the west side of Interstate 15 east to Paradise Road.

Completed in 1995, the $13 million Strip Beautification Project was a major renovation, beautification and upgrade of Las Vegas Boulevard South in the resort corridor from Hacienda Avenue to Sahara Avenue. The project dramatically enhanced the Strips appearance and streetscape. This 4.5 mile section of Las Vegas Boulevard is now designated a Nevada Scenic Byway.

Being one of the busiest streets in the nation, pedestrian traffic on Las Vegas Boulevard was dangerous to say the least. In 2012 the Nevada Department of Transportation estimated that the intersection of Las Vegas Boulevard and Tropicana Avenue had an annual average daily traffic flow of roughly a quarter million vehicles! Pedestrians hampered traffic flow at all intersections. Pedestrians and drivers were distracted taking in the sights, some overtired and some possibly intoxicated, creating a dangerous mix. Although these conditions still exist and human nature doesn't change, the gradual addition of elevated crosswalks at the Strip's major intersections greatly added to the streets aesthetics, improved traffic flow, and provides greater safety for pedestrian traffic.

♠♥♣♦

There are five locations on Las Vegas Boulevard serviced by elevated crosswalks connecting casino properties. Each crosswalk can be accessed by stairs, escalators and elevators (unless out of service for maintenance, which occurs more often than might be expected):

1 • Tropicana Avenue Crosswalks •
Between the Excalibur ↔ New York-New York ↔ MGM Grand ↔ Tropicana ↔ Excalibur

2 • City Center ↔ Planet Hollywood Crosswalk •
Between Planet Hollywood ↔ The Cosmopolitan ↔ Aria

3 • Flamingo Road Crosswalks •
Between the Bellagio ↔ Caesars Palace ↔ The Cromwell ↔ Bally's ↔ Bellagio

4 • Venetian ↔ Mirage/TI Crosswalk•

5 • Sands & Spring Mountain Avenue Crosswalks •
Between TI (Treasure Island) ↔ Fashion Show Mall ↔ Wynn ↔ Venetian

♠♥♣♦

The first set of crosswalks was constructed in 1994 at the intersection of Tropicana Avenue, Las Vegas' busiest intersection. Today it is estimated that 130,000 people a day use the bridges to access the Excalibur, New York-New York, MGM Grand and Tropicana!

A $30 million upgrade of the Tropicana Pedestrian Bridges commenced in mid-2016. The project will replace all 16 escalators with new state-of-the-art equipment, install new low energy glass and air-conditioning units in the elevators, and aesthetic bridge improvements that include tempered glass wind screens, polished aluminum cladding and lighted hand railings. All crosswalk bridge enhancements were scheduled to be completed by mid-2018, but the project is running ahead of schedule. During construction three crosswalks will always remain open to foot traffic.

Improvements commenced with Phase 1 the Tropicana ↔ Excalibur crosswalk, which has been completed and reopened to foot traffic. Phase 2 the Tropicana ↔ MGM Grand crosswalk, has been completed and reopened to foot traffic. Phase 3 the MGM Grand ↔ New York-New York crosswalk, is currently closed to foot traffic and scheduled to reopen at the end of September 2017. Work on Phase 4, the New York-New York ↔ Excalibur crosswalk, is scheduled from July 2017 to December 2017 and will be closed to foot traffic from the end of September.

♠♥♣♦

Las Vegas, known worldwide as a major tourist destination, offers nearly 150,000 hotel rooms. The Strip is home to the world's largest concentration of casino/hotel properties. Also, twenty-one of the world's forty largest hotels (by room count) are located on the Strip, which by itself boasts over 62,000 rooms!

In years past, when the majority of casino properties were independently owned and operated, market conditions existed that created a great deal of competition. Today, with but a handful of corporate entities controlling most major casino properties in the Las Vegas valley, there is still competition, but not on as great a scale. After all, it would be counterproductive to compete with yourself! In consequence, overall prices have increased and even though they still exist, deals and bargains have become harder to locate.

Strip casino resorts are basically divided between two major operators: MGM Resorts International owns and operates most of the west side of the Strip from Spring Mountain Road to Sunset Road; while the east side is saturated with Caesars Entertainment properties:

MGM Resorts International operates the following properties: Aria; Bellagio; Circus Circus; Excaliber; Luxor; Mandalay Bay; THE Hotel at Mandalay Bay; Mandarin Oriental; MGM Grand; Sign at the MGM Grand; The Mirage; Monte Carlo; New York-New York and Vdara. All hotels can be accessed through **www.mgmresorts.com** or property specific website listed in the Lodging section of this guide.

Caesars Entertainment (Previously Harrah's Entertainment) operates: Bally's; Caesars Palace; The Cromwell; Flamingo; Harrah's; Paris; Planet Hollywood; The LINQ Resort & Casino and The Rio. All hotels can be accessed through **www.caesars.com** or property specific website.

The remainder of the Strip resorts are owned and operated individually or in pairs:

Wynn Resorts Ltd. operates the Wynn and Encore. **www.wynnresorts.com**.

Las Vegas Sands Corporation operates The Venetian and Palazzo. **www.lasvegassands.com**.

American Casino & Entertainment Properties operates the Stratosphere Tower Casino & Resort Hotel; and has two off-Strip properties: Arizona Charlie's Decatur and Arizona Charlie's Boulder. The sale of all three properties to **Golden Entertainment** is pending. Incidentally, the Stratosphere is the only major Strip resort actually situated within Las Vegas city limits! All hotels can be accessed through **www.acepllc.com** or property specific website.

Penn National Gaming Inc. operates The M Resort Spa Casino and the Tropicana Casino Resort. Property specific website or **www.pngaming.com**

Michael Gaughan owns and operates the South Point Hotel Casino & Spa. **www.southpointcasino.com**

Phil Ruffin owns and operates the TI (Treasure Island). **www.treasureisland.com**

Starwood Hotels & Resorts owns and operates SLS Hotel & Casino. Property recently sold to the **Meruelo Group** and is pending regulatory approval. **www.slslasvegas.com**

Blackstone Real Estate Partners VII, a division of the New York City based Blackstone Group, own and operate The Cosmopolitan of Las Vegas. **www.cosmopolitanlasvegas.com**

Also evident on the Strip is a great deal of resort construction activity, or inactivity as the case may be! On the southern end of the Strip the site where the Hotel at Harmon was torn down, before ever being used, sits vacant.

The unfinished Fontainebleau, purchased in bankruptcy by Carl Icahn and up for sale, sits idle awaiting a new buyer to complete construction. As usual, rumors abound that a sale could be imminent.

The old Stardust property (construction site of Boyd Gaming's Echelon Place, mothballed in 2008 and sold to the Genting Group in 2013) also sits idle awaiting the stalled Resorts World Las Vegas project. When or if built, this Chinese themed resort could be one of the last "themed" resorts in Las Vegas. (MGM Resorts is in the process of de-theming properties.)

Just across the street, the Riviera (purchased by the Las Vegas Convention and Visitors Authority in 2015) was imploded and demolished in June and August of 2016, clearing way for the proposed Las Vegas Global Business District.

When these projects reach completion, someday, hopefully sooner than later, the northern section of Las Vegas Boulevard will become as vibrant as the southern!

Market conditions at off-Strip and Downtown properties produce greater competition. In consequence, casino owners and operators in these areas generally offer lower rates than Strip properties. Again, these properties are mainly controlled by a few entities:

Boyd Gaming operates Aliante Casino & Hotel; Cannery Casino & Hotel; Eastside Cannery Casino & Hotel; Orleans Hotel & Casino; Gold Coast Hotel & Casino; Suncoast Hotel & Casino; Sam's Town Hotel & Gambling Hall; California Hotel Casino; Fremont Hotel & Casino and Main Street Station Casino Brewery Hotel. Can be accessed through property specific websites or **www.boydgaming.com**

In 2016 Boyd Gaming purchased the Aliante Casino & Hotel for $380 million. Aliante was built by Station Casinos at a cost of $662 million, opened in 2008 and was turned over to creditors during bankruptcy in 2011. The property is currently undergoing the transition into the Boyd Group. **www.aliantecasinohotel.com**

Boyd Gaming also purchased both Cannery Casino Resorts from Millennium Gaming Inc. & Crown Limited for a total of $230 million. The Eastside Cannery **www.eastsidecannery.com** and Cannery Casino Hotel **www.cannerycasino.com** were built at a cost of $350 million. The transitioning and rebranding of these properties into the Boyd group is under way.

Red Rock Resorts is the corporate name of the holding company created by **Station Casinos** when the company went public in April. Property branding is not changing, and Station Casinos will remain the operating company for Boulder Station Hotel & Casino; Sunset Station Hotel & Casino; Santa Fe Station Hotel & Casino; Texas Station Gaming Hall & Hotel; Palace Station Hotel & Casino; Green Valley Ranch Resort Casino & Spa; Red Rock Casino Resort & Spa; Days Inn & Wild Wild West Gambling Hall; Fiesta Henderson; and Fiesta Rancho. All properties can be accessed through **www.sclv.com** or property specific website.

Flush with cash from an IPO offering, Red Rock Resorts purchased the Palms Casino Resort in 2016 from TPG Capital (parent company of Caesars Entertainment 49%), Leonard Green & Partners (49%) and the Maloof family (2% - the Maloof's lost control of the property in 2011) for $312.5 million. The transitioning and rebranding of the Palms into the Stations group is under way. **www.palms.com**

Affinity Gaming LLC operates Silver Seven's Hotel & Casino in Las Vegas; Buffalo Bills Resort & Casino, Primm Valley Resort & Casino and Whiskey Pete's Hotel & Casino in Primm Nevada (Stateline at the border of Nevada and California on I-15). All hotels can be accessed through **www.affinitygamingllc.com** or property specific website.

♠♥♣♦

In addition to Boyd Gaming, previously mentioned with three Downtown properties, there are six other casino operators in Downtown Las Vegas.

Derek and Gregory Stevens own and operate The D and Golden Gate. The Stevens brothers will play an even larger role in the modernization and future of Fremont Street gaming with their 2016 purchases of the shuttered Las Vegas Club Hotel & Casino and the buildings that housed Glitter Gulch, Mermaids and La Bayou (all now closed). The block is proposed to become the future home of the Stevens' third Downtown hotel/casino property.

TLC Casino Enterprises (Terry L. Caudill) owns and operates the Four Queens and Binion's. Harrah's Entertainment owned Binion's just long enough to strip it of the Horseshoe name and the World Series of Poker franchise, reselling Binion's to MTR Gaming Group. Binion's was acquired from MTR by TLC for $32 million in January 2008. Since December 2009 the hotel rooms have remained closed to the public.

Landry's Inc. owns and operates the Golden Nugget, which explains the property's dining options; a 24-hour Claim Jumper restaurant, a Chart House, Grotto, Lillie's, and Vic & Anthony's Steakhouse!

Tamares Group, a global private investment group, owns and operates the Plaza.

CIM Group, an urban real estate and infrastructure fund, owns the Downtown Grand, which is operated by Fifth Street Gaming.

Kenney Epstein owns and operates the El Cortez, the last remaining stand-alone Downtown casino/hotel located further than a block away from the Fremont Street Experience.

♠♥♣♦

Once you've determined whether to stay at a property Downtown, on the Strip or off-Strip; whether you'll be utilizing public transportation, shuttles, taxis, driving, bicycling or walking in Vegas; consider the weather. Remember also that distances can be deceiving in the desert. What may appear to be a few buildings away on the Strip, can actually be many miles distant! Walking or waiting for public transportation in the cold, heat or rain of the Las Vegas valley can be miserable!

When packing, take into consideration that valley weather can be extreme. For when it is cold it is a bitter, with biting cold winds blowing through the snowcapped mountains surrounding the valley! It is not uncommon to have at least one winter morning when a trace of snow covers the ground throughout the valley, but you would never know it by midday! The highest monthly snowfall recorded was in January 1949, a whopping 16.7 inches!

Historically, the coldest months of the year are December and January. The lowest minimum temperature on record, 8° Fahrenheit, was recorded January 13, 1963 and January 25, 1937.

On the other hand, when it is hot in the Las Vegas valley it can stay hot! National Weather Service records reveal that on average Las Vegas experiences seventy days of temperatures over 100° F every year! In fact, June 2015 was officially the hottest ever! More than half of the month was at or above 105° F, with an average temperature of 91.9° F! For the second year in a row, June 2016 broke the previous record with an average temperature of 92.5° F!

Historically, the hottest months are July and August. The highest maximum temperature ever recorded, 117° F, was reached on June 20, 2017, June 30, 2013, July 19, 2005 and July 24, 1942.

The Las Vegas valley's monthly normal average low/high temperature, based on the period from 1981 to 2010 and expressed in degrees Fahrenheit, follows:

- Jan   39°/58°
- Feb   43°/63°
- Mar   49°/70°
- Apr   56°/78°
- May   66°/89°
- Jun   75°/99°
- Jul   81°/104°
- Aug   79°/102°
- Sep   71°/94°
- Oct   59°/81°
- Nov   47°/66°
- Dec   39°/57°

For further Las Vegas weather information check out this National Weather Service publication:

www.wrh.noaa.gov/vef/climate/LasVegasClimateBook/ind
ex.php

♠♥♣♦

On a final preparatory note, throughout this guide you will come across references to discounts for locals. In general these offers merely require a Nevada ID, although some also require a local address. If you are moving to Las Vegas, change your driver's license or obtain a Nevada ID as soon as possible in order to take advantage of great promotional discounts for locals!

Unlike most other states (if not all), the State of Nevada provides a method to obtain a local ID for tourists that temporarily reside in the state (for a period of at least 31 consecutive days)! Although you cannot hold both an Identification Card and a Driver License (even if they are from different states), Nevada offers a **Seasonal Resident ID Card**! Seasonal resident identification cards are marked with a designation that the holder is a seasonal resident and is licensed in another state (these cards are not issued to tourists from foreign countries).

- **Nevada Department of Motor Vehicles** -
www.dmvnv.com/idcards.htm
- Local 702.486.4368 (702.486.4DMV) -

Part year Nevada resident ID

The residency and proof of identity requirements for a Nevada identification card are the same as those for a driver license. To apply for an original Nevada Identification Card, you must: provide acceptable proof of your identity; provide a valid Nevada street address; apply in person at a DMV office; complete a Driver License Application (DMV 002); pay the required fee (18 through 64 = $22.25, 65 or older = $8.25); present any existing U.S. driver license, permit or ID card; and have your picture taken.

TRANSPORTATION

According to the annual visitor survey of the Las Vegas Convention Authority, 57% of all visitors arrive by ground transportation and only 43% arrive by air. In 2015, more than half (53%) of Las Vegas visitors were from the western United States, with the bulk of them (29%) coming from California.

♠♥♣♦

Traveling by car

Las Vegas is located on Interstate 15 between Los Angeles (270 miles ± to the southwest) and Salt Lake City (420 miles ± to the northeast). Phoenix is to the southeast, roughly 290 miles via US Highway 93.

When traveling by car to Las Vegas, especially to and from California via I-15, stay alert and use more caution than normal. Many drivers headed to Las Vegas are in a hurry to get there, excessive speeding is commonplace. On the return trip drivers are apt to be overtired, hungover, or in the worst case scenario, driving under the influence.

Based on a 2009 study of the top ten roads with most fatalities over the past five years by county, I-15 is one of the deadliest strips of highway in the United States. San Bernardino County in California ranked number one, with 346 fatalities. Ranked sixth was Clark County Nevada, with 148 fatalities. Since then, many improvements have been made to the Interstate. Between the state line (Primm, NV.) and Las Vegas for example, cement barriers have been added dividing northbound and southbound lanes, helping prevent crossovers and head-on collisions.

Driving & Parking in Las Vegas

Whether driving your own car or a rental in Las Vegas, you should consider that gas prices will typically be higher nearer the Strip. There is a website that provides the location of the lowest priced gasoline near your location. Simply enter one of the zip codes provided in the lodging listings at **www.vegasgasprices.com**.

When driving, remember that the Strip will be slow going, clogged with traffic and sightseers. The best way to bypass the Strip traffic is by using the north/south service roads; Koval Lane and Paradise Road to the east of the Strip; Frank Sinatra Drive, Dean Martin Drive and Industrial Road to the west.

If you're headed east or west of the Strip driving can be made difficult dependent on the time of day and direction, due to facing into the sun, the cause of many accidents. The best east/west road to skip the Strip traffic jams, especially during rush hours, is East Desert Inn Road, the Strip by-pass. Built in the mid-1990s, this two mile limited access "Super Arterial" will get you back and forth from Paradise Road in the east to South Valley View Boulevard in the west, within minutes! The route is nonstop, going over Interstate 15 and under Las Vegas Boulevard.

♠♥♣♦

One of the greatest bargains in Las Vegas, or perk for the frugal minded, has always been the availability of ample free parking. For those who preferred not to make that long trek from the parking lot or garage into the casino, you could slip a few dollars to the valet and step straight into an air conditioned lobby! Unfortunately, the trend in Las Vegas has been to implement fees, charging for what has traditionally been free!

In June 2016 free parking as a perk began to vanish from the Vegas Strip when MGM Resorts International implemented the policy of charging for valet and self-parking at all of its properties. Just as with the unpopular Resort Fee, in the short term MGM's competitors refrained from implementing their own parking fees. However, with MGM Resorts leading the way and raking in millions, it took a mere six months for Caesars Entertainment, Wynn Resorts and The Cosmopolitan to begin charging parking fees. Twenty-six Strip properties now charge some form of parking fee.

• MGM Resorts Parking •
www.mgmresorts.com/parking

Self-Parking Rates:
- 0 to 1 hour • Complimentary (1st Day Only) •
- 1 to 2 hours * • $5 or $7 •
- 2 to 4 hours * • $8, $10 or $12 •
- 4 to 24 hours * • $10, $12 or $15 •
- Over 24 hrs * • $10, $12 or $15 per day or portion thereof •

Valet Parking Rates:
- 0 to 4 hours * • $10, $15 or $20 •
- 4 to 24 hours *• $15, $20 or $25 •
- Over 24 hrs *• $15, $20 or $25 per day or portion thereof •

*Rate varies dependent on property.

TIPS: Mlife Rewards Pearl, Gold, Platinum and NOIR members receive complimentary self-parking. Valet parking is complimentary for Gold, Platinum and NOIR members. Self-parking is free for everyone at Circus Circus. One of the perks of the MLife Mastercard, (Frugal Gaming chapter) is free self-parking at MGM Resorts properties.

• Caesars Entertainment Parking •
www.caesars.com/parking

Self-Parking Rates:
- 0 to 1 hour • Complimentary •
- 1 to 4 hours * • $5 or $7 •
- 4 to 24 hours *• $8 or $10 •
- Over 24 hours * • $8 or $10 per day or portion thereof •

Valet Parking Rates:
- 0 to 4 hours * •$8 or $13 •
- 4 to 24 hours * • $13 or $18 •
- Over 24 hours * • $13 or $18 per day or portion thereof •

*Rate varies dependent on property.

TIPS: Self-parking and valet is free for Total Rewards Platinum, Diamond and Seven Stars members. Nevada residents must pay for valet, but can self-park for free up to 24 hours. One of the perks of the Total Rewards Visa Card (Frugal Gaming chapter) is free self-parking at Caesars Entertainment properties.

• Wynn Resorts Parking •
www.wynnlasvegas.com/AboutUs/Directions

Self-parking: Garages located at Wynn and Encore remain free of charge for guests at this time, but the resorts have not clarified whether free self-parking will be permanent or re-evaluated at a later date.

Valet Parking Rates:
- 0 to 4 hours • $13 •
- 4 to 24 hours • $18 •
- Over 24 hours • $18 per day or portion thereof •

• The Cosmopolitan of Las Vegas Parking •
www.cosmopolitanlasvegas.com/parking

Self-Parking Rates:
- 0 to 1 hour • Complimentary •
- 1 to 4 hours • $7 •
- 4 to 24 hours • $10 •
- Over 24 hours • $10 per day or portion thereof •

Valet Parking Rates:
- 0 to 4 hours • $13 •
- 4 to 24 hours • $18 •
- Over 24 hours • $18 per day or portion thereof •

TIPS: Free Valet parking for Identity members Gold status or higher subject to availability. Free self-parking for Identity members Sterling status or higher. Motorcycles and two-wheeled vehicles are exempt from self-parking fees.

• TI (Treasure Island) Parking •

Valet and self-parking is free for registered hotel guests. Non-hotel guests can use the self-parking garage at the rate of $2 per hour. Self-parking for up to 4 hours is also complimentary based on your casino play.

NOTE: Policy may have changed. TI website indicates "Valet & Self-Parking Garage Always Free."

• Free Self-Parking Options •

If you're not in a hurry and don't mind a short walk or a free shuttle ride, let's face it many parking garages are a long walk to the casino anyway, there still remain many properties with free self-parking options:

• RIO • Circus Circus • SLS Las Vegas • The Venetian & Palazzo • Tropicana • Stratosphere • Casino Royal • The Fashion Show Mall • Lucky Dragon • Palace Station • Palms • Tuscany • Westin • Hooters • Hard Rock • Ellis Island • Silver Sevens • Gold Coast • Orleans • Sam's Town • Westgate •

♠♥♣♦

Traveling by train

Amtrak's "Desert Wind" provided regularly scheduled service between Los Angeles and Salt Lake City, with a stop in Downtown Las Vegas, sadly the "Desert Wind' was discontinued in 1997. Today, Las Vegas is not serviced by passenger rail. Amtrak's closest stop to Las Vegas is in Kingman, Arizona, on the route of the "Southwest Chief."

It is said that Amtrak offers a shuttle to Las Vegas from Kingman, but this cannot be confirmed. A recent search indicates that a Greyhound bus ticket from Kingman to Las Vegas ranges from $18 to $35 dependent upon how many days in advance the ticket is purchased.

♠♥♣♦

Traveling by bus

The major nationwide bus line, Greyhound, provides extensive daily service to and from Las Vegas. The bus station is conveniently located Downtown next to the Plaza Hotel & Casino.

• Greyhound Bus Lines •
www.greyhound.com
• Toll Free 800.231.2222 •

Greyhound offers discounts for companions, students, military & veterans, seniors, groups of 7 or more, and for midweek travel. Bus tickets can be purchased online or at any station, but cheaper fares require a 14 day advance purchase (New York to Las Vegas as low as $129 with advance purchase).

♠♥♣♦

Las Vegas also has extensive bus service from two low cost carriers specifically servicing the Las Vegas market. Both advertise fares as low as $1!

• BoltBus •
www.boltbus.com
•Toll Free 877.265.8287 •

BoltBus is owned by Greyhound Lines, Inc. and has two stops in Las Vegas, one at Bay 10 of the RTC South Strip Transfer Terminal, the other at 500 South 1st Street near the RTC Bonneville Station Downtown. From Las Vegas, BoltBus serves Barstow, Hollywood, Los Angeles, and Ontario, California. A recent search showed numerous fares in the low $20 range from Las Vegas to Union Station in Los Angeles.

♠♥♣♦

• Megabus •
www.megabus.com
• Toll Free 877.462.6342 • $7 phone reservation fee •

Megabus, Greyhounds largest competitor, has only one Las Vegas drop-off and pick-up point, also at the RTC South Strip Transfer Terminal. From Las Vegas, Megabus serves Anaheim, Los Angeles, and Riverside, California. Megabus fares must be booked online, but typically seem to offer a wider range of fares lower than BoltBus fares. For the same dates BoltBus fares were researched, Megabus fares were less than half.

♠♥♣♦

• LuxXpress •
www.luxxpress.com
• Toll Free 888.800.8003 •

LuxXpress offers pricier multiple daily bus transportation services between Las Vegas and Los Angeles, Anaheim, Garden Grove and the Diamond Bar areas of California for $40 one-way or $70 round-trip. The Vegas pick-up and drop-off point is at the Gold Coast on Flamingo Road.

♠♥♣♦

Traveling by air

For the frugal traveler the nation's two largest discount carriers, Allegiant Air and Spirit Airlines, offer service to and from McCarran International Airport. I will not go into the pros or cons of traveling by a discount carrier, some people hate them, while others like myself, have never had an issue flying with them. If you're worried about leg room, at the gate ask politely for a seat on the isle (or volunteer for an emergency exit seat, these are almost always available at gate check-in). If you do not wish to fly a discount airline, many other airlines offer service to and from McCarran.

♠♥♣♦

• McCarran International Airport (LAS) •
www.mccarran.com

- Flight Information • Local 702.261.4636 •
- Parking Information • Local 702.261.5121 •
- General Information • Local 702.261.5211 •
- TDD • Local 702.261.3111 •
- Paging • Local 702.261.5211 •
- Lost & Found • Local 702.261.5134 •

McCarran Airport consists of 110 aircraft gates at two separate terminal buildings, each with its own parking garage, ticketing/check-in area, baggage claim, shops, and dining options. The two facilities are not physically connected, so it is important you know which airline operates out of which terminal building. If you end up at the wrong terminal, McCarran Airport provides a courtesy **inter-terminal shuttle** between Terminal 1 and Terminal 3 with stops located on Ground Level Zero.

<u>Terminal 1</u> includes a 6000 space parking garage and a spacious terminal building with Ticketing/Check-in, Baggage Claim, and the A, B and C Gates. The D Gates satellite concourse is accessible from Terminal 1 via an automated transit system. Terminal 1 features a variety of shopping, dining, and services. All airlines operating at the A, B, C and D Gates share one baggage claim on Level 1 of Terminal 1. **Allegiant**, **American**, **Delta**, **Omni**, **Southwest** and **Spirit Airlines** operate out of this terminal.

McCarran International Airport

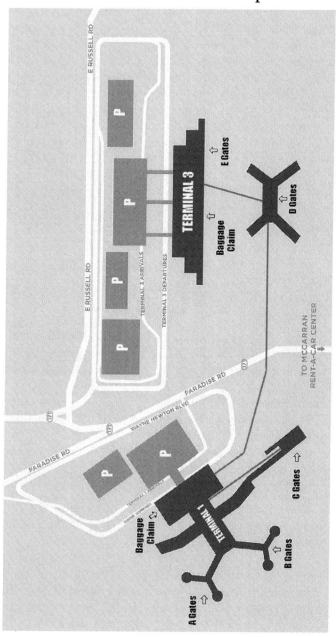

In June 2012 Terminal 2 was permanently closed. Terminal 3, a new 14-gate terminal, opened on June 27, 2012.

Terminal 3 is home to all foreign flag carriers and some domestic carriers. Features include a Ticketing/Check-in area, Baggage Claim, a Customs & Border Protection arrivals hall, duty free store, plus a variety of shopping and dining options.

The following airlines operate from Terminal 3; **International Airlines**: Aeromexico, **Air Canada**, **British Airways**, **Condor**, **COPA Airlines**, Edelweiss, Interiet, **Korean Air**, **MagniCharters**, **Norwegian**, **Sunwing**, **Thomas Cook**, **Virgin Atlantic**, **VivaAerobus**, **Volaris**, and WestJet. **Domestic Airlines:** Alaska, **Frontier**, **Hawaiian**, JetBlue, **Sun Country**, **United** and **Virgin America**.

Renting a car

There are numerous options for renting a vehicle in Las Vegas. You can rent a car at the airport, on-site at many casino/hotel properties, or at standalone agencies scattered throughout the valley. The easiest method would be to rent at the airport for your entire stay. As in any major city though, renting at the airport is more expensive due to higher rental rates and airport fees.

Taking into considering traffic congestion and parking fees, having constant access to a car during your stay may not be required. Las Vegas is a city where tourists have many low cost transportation options available to them. Unless you plan on extensive driving, consider other transportation options. If you desire, you can always rent a car for a day trip and save the expense of a rental for your entire visit.

If you still feel that you must have a rental car, the McCarran Rent-A-Car Center is located at 7135 Gilespie Street, three miles from the airport near the South Strip Transfer Terminal (city bus terminal), with easy access to Interstates 215 & 15 and the Strip.

♠♥♣♦
• McCarran Rent-A-Car Center •
www.mccarran.com/Go/RentalCars.aspx
• Local 702.261.6001 •

The McCarran Rent-A-Car Center is open 24 hours and is served by the following car rental agencies:

- **Advantage Rent A Car** • **www.advantage.com**
- Toll Free 800.777.9377 •

- **Alamo** • **www.alamo.com**
- Toll Free 800.462.5266 •

- **Avis** • **www.avis.com**
Toll Free 800.331.1212 •

- **Budget** • **www.budget.com**
- Toll Free 800.922.2899 •

- **Dollar** • **www.dollar.com**
- Toll Free 800.800.4000 •

- **E-Z Rent-A-Car** • **www.ezrentacar.com**
- Toll Free 800.277.5171 •

- **Enterprise** • **www.enterprise.com**
- Toll Free 800.736.7222 •

- **Firefly Car Rental** • **www.fireflycarrental.com**
- Toll Free 888.296.9135 •

- **Hertz** • **www.hertz.com**
- Toll Free 800.654.3131 •

- **National** • **www.nationalcar.com**
- Toll Free 800.227.7368 •

- **Payless Car Rental** • **www.paylesscarrental.com**
- Toll Free 800.729.5377 •

- **Thrifty** • **www.thrifty.com**
- Toll Free 800.367.2277 •

- **zipcar** • **www.zipcar.com**
- Toll Free 800.494.7227 •

♠♥♣♦

If you have reservations with an off-site rental car agency that is not listed above, contact the company directly for additional information or specific pick-up instructions. Typically, off-site rental agencies pick-up at Space 4 located by the taxicab staging area at the McCarran Rent-A-Car Center.

Arriving car rental customers will be transported to the McCarran Rent-A-Car Center in blue and white shuttle buses, which depart approximately every five minutes for the three-mile trip to the center and the car rental agency of their choice.

Rental Car Pick-up from Terminal 1

From Baggage Claim, follow signs to Ground Transportation on Level 1. Proceed to the Rental Car Shuttle located at the center median outside doors 10 and 11.

Rental Car Pick-up from Terminal 3

Follow signs to Ground Transportation from Baggage Claim on Level Zero. Proceed to the Rental Car Shuttle located outside West doors 51↔54 and East doors 55↔58.

Rental Car Return

Upon arrival at the McCarran Rent-A-Car Center, follow the signs to the Rental Car Return entrance off Gilespie Street. Follow the overhead signs to the appropriate car rental company. After returning your vehicle, proceed through the lobby and out the main entrance to the shuttles. Blue and white shuttle buses depart for the airport approximately every five minutes. Board the appropriate shuttle to either Terminal 1 or Terminal 3 for your departing flight.

♠♥♣♦
Taxicab

Sixteen taxicab companies service the Las Vegas Valley and each has their own color scheme to assist in differentiating the specific company. Taxicab service is regulated by the Nevada Taxicab Authority, a Nevada State agency responsible for issuing medallions and setting fares. Taxicab Authority enforcement personnel are on duty 24 hours a day, 365 days a year. Contact the Dispatch Office if you require assistance at: 702.668.4000 • **www.taxi.nv.gov**

Passengers arriving at **Terminal 1** will find taxicabs available on the east side of baggage claim, outside door exits 1↔4. Airport personnel are available to help queue the lines and provide assistance as needed.

Passengers arriving at **Terminal 3** will find taxicabs located outside on Level Zero. There are twenty taxi loading positions on the west end of the building to serve domestic travelers and ten loading positions on the east side of the building to accommodate international travelers. Airport personnel are available to assist as needed.

♠♥♣♦

A few pointers when using a taxi in Las Vegas:

• Fares must be paid in U.S. currency. Some taxicabs are cash only and do not accept credit card payments. Customers should notify the attendant if they plan to use a credit card for payment. Passengers utilizing a credit card for payment will be charged a $3 fee over and above the meter charge.

• Taxicab passengers cannot be charged for the loading/unloading or transporting of their luggage. Tips or gratuities to taxi drivers in Las Vegas are optional and not required. A taxicab passenger in Las Vegas must be given a completed receipt if they request one.

• The maximum number of passengers allowed in any taxi is five, including infants and children. Unlike most US cities, flagging or hailing a ride in Las Vegas is not allowed. Taxicab drivers cannot legally pick-up passengers off of the street. The airport, casinos, hotels, malls, clubs, and some businesses & restaurants, all have taxicab stands.

• A tunnel and road was built under the runways at the airport, which takes you to I-215 just south of the airport and connects with I-15. Dependent on traffic, use of the Airport Tunnel to I-215 may provide a quicker route to your destination. However, remember that the tunnel from

McCarran Airport is not the shortest route to any Strip hotel! Taking the tunnel will result in a higher fare. The tunnel would be the best route to exit the airport <u>only</u> if your destination is located southeast, south or southwest of the airport (ie…South Point, Silverton, M Resort, Green Valley Ranch, Sunset Station).

● As a matter of law, taxicab drivers must obey the passenger's directions as it relates to the route taken: "Your driver may not take a longer route to your destination than is necessary, unless specifically requested by the passenger (NRS 706.8846)."

When a taxi driver takes the least direct route (airport tunnel for example) without the passenger's permission, the crime of long hauling occurs. If you find yourself in a cab leaving the airport through a tunnel, and you did not specifically request taking the tunnel or quickest route, you are probably being long hauled!

● **FARES**: When you enter a taxicab, the driver will start the taximeter (referred to as the "drop") and an initial charge of $3.50 will register. If a taxi ride <u>originates</u> at McCarran International Airport, an additional airport surcharge of $2 per trip is added to the meter. After the initial "drop", the meter will assess a fare of $2.76 per mile (23¢ for each 1/12th of a mile traveled). If the meter senses that the taxicab is moving less than 8↔12 MPH, the meter will assess a charge of 25¢ (twenty-five cents) every 30 seconds ($32.40 per hour waiting time). That is why the meter continues to accumulate charges even when the taxicab is not moving. Once the meter senses that the taxicab is moving at a speed greater than 8↔12 MPH the fare calculates on the actual distance traveled. A 3% excise tax is added to all rates and fees.

● Check the hotel listings later in this guide for approximate minimum rate information utilizing service streets from McCarran Airport to Las Vegas Strip Hotels. Fares may vary depending on time of day, day of week, route taken,

destination, weather, road conditions, and traffic. The fares in this guide were calculated using:
www.taxifarefinder.com

• Remember that the Strip will be slow going, clogged with traffic and sightseers. Unless you desire to become one of those sightseers, the fastest and best way to bypass the Strip traffic is by using the north/south service roads. Dependent on your destination, ask your driver to use either Koval Lane or Paradise Road to the east of the Strip; Frank Sinatra Drive, Dean Martin Drive or Industrial Road to the west.

• In the event you forget something in a taxi, call the company immediately. All taxicab companies are required to maintain a lost-and found for items left in cabs. If you cannot remember the name of the cab company, the Nevada Taxicab Authority has photos of all companies color schemes on its website for identification purposes.

• **A-Cab Company** • 702.365.1900 •

• **ANLV/Ace/Union/Vegas-Western/Virgin Valley Cab Companies** • 702.888.4888 •

• **Checker/Yellow/Star Cab Company** • 702.873.2000 •

• **Deluxe Cab Company** • 702.568.7700 •

• **Desert Cab Company** • 702.386.4828 •

• **Henderson Taxi** • 702.384.2322 •

• **Lucky Cab Company** • 702.477.7555 •

• **Nellis Cab Company** • 702.248.1111 •

• **Western Cab Company** • 702.736.8000 •

• **Whittlesea Blue Cab Company** • 702.384.6111•

♠♥♣♦
Personal Car Services

Growing in popularity, nationwide personal car driving services Uber and Lyft are available in Las Vegas. Due to having no overhead (drivers use their personal cars) these companies offer fares about half that of a taxi. If two or more people are traveling together, these services are even cheaper than a paid shuttle. Both companies offer ride sharing options (UberPOOL & Lyft Line) and sign-up promotions!

Completely cashless (utilizes credit or debit card on file), fare quotes, reservations, pick-up and payment are all handled with the tap of a mobile app! On the upside; you don't have to wait in a taxi line, worry about getting long-hauled, you know the fare before getting in the car, and there is not a credit or debit card surcharge. On the downside there is Uber Surge Pricing and Lyft PrimeTime Pricing, busy periods when rates are temporarily increased.

According to the expense management firm Certify, between early 2014 and early 2016 the average Uber ride cost was $26.41, while the average taxi fare was $39.68. Over the same period Lyft was even cheaper at just $23.53 per ride.

TIP: In addition to utilizing Uber or Lyft's fare estimation webpages listed below, for a quick fare comparison you can also visit **www.fareestimate.com**.

Uber and Lyft both offer Airport pick-up:
Terminal 1, Public Parking Garage, Level 2M.
Terminal 3, Parking Garage, Valet Level.

● **Uber** ●
www.uber.com/cities/las-vegas

The industry creator, Uber's rates are calculated as follows: a $1.90 booking fee, base fee of $1.50, plus 90¢ per mile, 15¢ per minute, 3% Nevada transportation tax and an airport pick-up/drop-off fee of $2.45 if applicable. Minimum fare is $6.90 and there is a $5 cancellation fee. A photo of the driver, car information and tracking are provided prior to pick-up. Uber advertises that there is no need to tip and a fare can be split among riders (no more freeloading friends)! Use promo code FEELING22 at sign-up for first trip free up to $22 (exp. 12/31/17). Codes change and should appear on sign-up page, if not, do a Google search for "Uber promotion codes."

• Lyft •
www.lyft.com/cities/las-vegas-nv

Lyft's rates are calculated as follows: a $1.90 service fee, base fee of $1.50, plus 90¢ per mile, 15¢ per minute, 3% Nevada transportation tax and an airport pick-up/drop-off fee of $2.45 if applicable. Minimum fare of $5.00 and there is a $5 cancellation fee. Even though the rates appear similar to Uber, based on fare quotes from both company's app's Lyft is cheaper (especially to the Strip). Currently Lyft is advertising new member sign-up codes 20LYFTPROMO ($2 credit per ride for 10 rides), NEWUSER10 ($5 credit per ride for 2 rides) or LYFTCOUPON9 ($3 credit per ride for 3 rides). Or do a Google search for "Lyft promotion codes."

TIP: It might be best to wait until you arrive in Vegas to sign-up, you may find that a better code is available. In the recent past, Lyft has been aggressively expanding Vegas market share with a $50 ride credit (5 rides $10 credit each) sign-up promotion. Codes were advertised in the airport, hotels, free tourist magazines and by hawkers on the Strip.

Paid Airport Shuttles

Numerous group shuttles operate to and from the airport, Strip or Downtown hotels. These services operate 24 hours a day, seven days a week and are an economical way to get from the airport to most major hotel/resorts. Dependent on passenger destinations, group shuttles make multiple stops en route. All shuttle services offer online booking in advance with a credit card, but it is not required. Walk up shuttle service with cash payment is also available. Driver gratuities are not included, but customary.

For **Terminal 1** arrivals, shuttles are available on the west side of baggage claim, outside door exits 7 to 13.

For **Terminal 3** arrivals, shuttles are located outside on Level Zero on the west end of the building to serve domestic travelers and on the east side of the building to accommodate international travelers.

• Airline Limousine •
www.airlineshuttlecorp.com
• Local 702.444.1234 • Toll Free 888.554.1156 •

Fares: Strip hotels $9 one-way, $15 round-trip; Downtown hotels $10 one-way, $18 round-trip. Offers a discount for active military and anyone over 60 (in-person only, not available online). Picks up at T1 just outside exit door #8. T3 (domestic), outside door #51.

• Bell Trans •
www.airportshuttlelasvegas.com
• Local 702.739.7990 • Toll Free 800.274.7433 •

Fares: Strip hotels $14 round-trip; Downtown hotels $17 round-trip. Picks up at T1 just outside exit door #9. T3 (domestic), outside exit door #52.

• Show Time Tours •
www.showtimetourslv.com
• Local 702.895.9976 • Toll Free 800.704.7011 •

Fares: Strip hotels $7.50 one-way, $14 round-trip; Downtown hotels $9 one-way, $18 round-trip. Picks up at T1 just outside exit door #10, T3 (domestic), outside exit door #52.

• Super Shuttle •
www.shuttlelasvegas.com
• Local 702.920.3186 • Toll Free 800.258.3826 •

Strip and Downtown hotels are a flat fare: $11 one-way or $20 round-trip. T1 check-in booth is just outside exit door #11, T3 check-in booth is inside baggage claim.

 # Free Airport Shuttles

Unfortunately there are no free airport shuttles to hotels on the Las Vegas Strip. It has been said that regulations prohibit individual hotels on the Strip from operating private shuttles to and from the airport. The reality is that all hotels in Las Vegas, including the Strip, are welcome to come to McCarran Airport and provide a shuttle service for their guests. There is no prohibition from doing this. However, like most other airports, there is a fee (to the operator) for any commercial ground transportation vehicles that come to the airport and pick-up arriving passengers, but there is no charge to drop-off passengers on the Departures Curb area. This is the reason why you will notice that some hotels offer a drop-off only airport shuttle.

Free shuttles pick-up from McCarran Airport at Ground Level Zero and most operate on a first come, first serve basis with limited seating. It is also recommended to set up a reservation with the hotel in advance for airport pickup. Being a free service, these shuttles often fill up fast, so plan to be at the pickup location early. All times are approximate and subject to change. Even if you happen to be first in line, priority boarding is typically granted to handicapped and upper tier level Players Club members. Tips are appreciated but not required.

- **Ellis Island/Super 8** advertises as a resort fee amenity, complimentary airport shuttle service 24 hours a day to hotel guests.

- **El Cortez Hotel & Casino** provides a complimentary shuttle from the hotel to the airport that is available, hourly 7 AM until 2 PM, Sunday through Friday. The hotel does not offer an airport pick-up service.

- **Green Valley Ranch Resort & Spa** provides a complimentary airport shuttle that picks up every two hours from 7:30 AM to 9:30 PM. The shuttle drops off at the departure level every two hours from 7 AM to 9 PM. For shuttle questions contact: 702.617.7745

- **M Resort** provides complimentary airport shuttle service on a set schedule. Shuttles pick-up at the airport from 6:30 AM until 9:30 PM. Shuttles to the airport depart at 6 AM until 9 PM. For shuttle questions contact: 702.797.1115

- **Mardi Gras Hotel & Casino** provides complimentary airport shuttle service daily from 7 AM to 10 PM. For shuttle questions contact: 702-731-2020

- **Palace Station Hotel & Casino** provides a complimentary airport shuttle service for guests only, on a set schedule.

Shuttles depart from the airport starting at 6:30 AM through 12 AM Schedule is available online:
www.palacestation.sclv.com/hotel

• **Plaza Hotel & Casino** advertises that the hotel now offers a free <u>drop off</u> transfer to the airport from the hotel on a set schedule. The hotel does not offer an airport pick-up service. Ask at the front desk for schedule or pricing for non-guests.

• **Red Rock Casino Resort & Spa** provides complimentary airport shuttle service for hotel guests. Shuttle picks up from ground zero at 6 AM and every two hours thereafter, through 8 PM. Last airport departure is at 9 PM. Shuttle departs Red Rock for the airport at 5 AM and every two hours thereafter. Last shuttle is at 7 PM.

• **Silver Sevens Hotel & Casino** provides complimentary airport shuttle service every hour from 4 AM until 12 AM.

• **Silverton Casino Hotel** provides complimentary scheduled shuttle service to and from the airport. Shuttles depart the airport for Silverton from 7:30 AM through 9:30 PM. Call 866.722.4608 for pick-up reservation.

• **South Point Hotel, Casino & Spa** provides complimentary airport shuttle service for hotel guests only. Shuttles pick-up at airport at 6:30 AM, 7:30 AM, 8:30 AM, 9:45 AM, 11 AM, 12:30 PM, 1:30 PM, 2:45 PM, 4:15 PM, 5:15 PM, 6:30 PM, 8 PM and 9:30 PM. Shuttles depart South Point for the airport at 6 AM, 7 AM, 8 AM, 9 AM, 10:15 AM, 11:45 AM, 1 PM, 2 PM, 3:30 PM, 4:45 PM, 5:45 PM, 7:15 PM and 8:45 PM.

• **Suncoast Hotel & Casino** provides complimentary airport shuttle service for hotel guests only. Shuttles pick-up at the airport every two hours on the hour starting at 9 AM, last shuttle at 7 PM. Shuttles depart Suncoast for the airport every two hours on the hour starting at 8 AM, last shuttle at 6 PM.

• **The Venetian & Palazzo** provide complimentary airport shuttle service for Club Grazie Gold & Platinum members plus one guest. Airport pick-up locations: Terminal 1 is outside door #9 and Terminal 3 is outside door #52.

♠♥♣♦

Regional Transit System (City Bus)

● Regional Transportation Commission (RTC) ●
www.rtcsnv.com
● Local 702.228.7433 ●

If you are traveling light with small easy to manage carryon bags, the RTC (city-wide bus system) has four routes that provide service to and from McCarran International Airport. You can get anywhere in the city by taking any of these routes and making a transfer to connecting bus routes. Two of these routes are express services with limited stops. Although extremely inexpensive for someone traveling light without time constraints, the RTC bus system may not be the easiest or most convenient way to get to most hotels from the airport. These are the available options:

● **Route 108 Paradise** departs from Terminal 1 Ground Zero Level roughly every thirty minutes from 4:56 AM through 1:25 AM. This service operates on a loop between the airport and Bonneville Transit Center Downtown, with stops about every quarter mile. There are stops near Westgate, SLS and Stratosphere. However, its northbound route is via Swenson and Desert Inn to Paradise, thereby by-passing the Mardi Gras, Silver Sevens and Hard Rock. To stop at these properties you would need to ride Downtown and then back on the southern return route.

● **Route 109 Maryland Parkway** provides frequent 24-hour service and departs from Terminal 1 Ground Zero Level. This route heads southbound to the South Strip Transfer Terminal (SSTT) where you can easily transfer to the **Strip & Downtown Express** which has stops at Mandalay Bay, MGM Grand, Paris, Wynn, SLS, Stratosphere, Bonneville Transit Center (BTC) and the Fremont Street Experience (servicing adjacent Downtown hotels). From midnight to 9 AM you can also transfer at the SSTT to the **Deuce on the Strip** route which is slower, but services more stops than the express. From the transfer terminal the 109 heads northbound to the Bonneville Transit Center (BTC) Downtown, with stops about every quarter mile.

• **Centennial Express (CX)** departs northbound from Terminal 3 Departures Level roughly once an hour on weekdays from 6:40 AM to 10:52 PM, and on weekends & holidays from 6:52 AM to 10:46 PM. The CX makes very few stops. Of interest to the traveler is the stop near the intersection of Las Vegas Boulevard (the Strip) with Sands Avenue & Spring Mountain Road. The hotels at this intersection are TI (Treasure Island), Wynn and Palazzo, but you can easily transfer to the southbound **Strip & Downtown Express (SDX)** or **Deuce on the Strip** which service other Strip properties. The CX continues from here a short distance on I-15 toward the Bonneville Transit Center (BTC). Its first stop after leaving the BTC is at 4th Street & Carson Avenue, a short block from Fremont Street Experience and the hotels located there.

• **Westcliff Airport Express (WAX)** departs from Terminal 3 Departures Level and stops at Terminal 1 Zero Level, then continues its northbound service. The WAX operates from the airport about once an hour (more often during peak hours) from 5:49 AM to 11:16 PM. <u>This is the cheapest and fastest way to the Strip or Downtown utilizing an RTC route</u>.

After departing the airport, the WAX makes two stops on Tropicana Avenue. The first stop is at Koval Lane, exit here for the MGM Grand, Hooters or the Tropicana. The second stop is just after Las Vegas Boulevard alongside New York-New York. Use this stop for the Excalibur as well. From here it's a short walk north to the Monte Carlo (Park MGM) and a short Tram ride to the Luxor and Mandalay Bay. You can also easily transfer to either the **Strip & Downtown Express (SDX)** or **Deuce on the Strip.**

The WAX then travels on northbound Interstate 15 for the quick trip Downtown and stops including Bonneville Transit Center (BTC) and 4th Street & Carson Avenue, the stop that services Fremont Street Experience and most Downtown hotels. The next and last Downtown stop is just after Stewart

Avenue, a short walk back to the Downtown Grand. From Downtown, the express heads to Summerlin where it has a stop in the Suncoast Hotel & Casino parking lot.

Routes **108**, **109** and **CX** do not provide service to both airport terminals. However, the airport operates a complimentary white & blue inter-terminal shuttle from Ground Level Zero.

If you are planning on getting around Las Vegas using the RTC bus system, the RTC publishes an easy to use *System Map*, *Transit Guide* and some individual route maps & schedules. Sometimes these are available on buses, but are always available at the Bonneville Transit Center (101 E. Bonneville Avenue - lobby hours 5 AM to 9 PM) and the South Strip Transfer Terminal (6675 Gilespie Street - lobby hours 6 AM to 10 PM). However, the easiest option is to view or download the *Transit Guide*, *System Map* and *Route Maps* for free! **https://www.rtcsnv.com/wp-content/uploads/routes/2016/2016-NovTransitGuide.pdf**

♠♥♣♦

There are numerous ways to purchase an RTC transit pass. If you have enough time you can order passes online to be delivered by US Mail (takes 7-10 days). You can purchase passes from an automated ticket vending machine (TVM), located at the airport bus stops, most Strip bus stops, and the South Strip Transfer Terminal. Keep in mind that TVM's accept credit and debit cards, as well as $1, $5, $10 and $20 bills, <u>but do not give change</u>!

You can purchase passes at the Bonneville Transit Center customer service booth Downtown, from 7:15 AM until 5:45 PM seven days a week. Passes can also be purchased at certain local vendors including Walgreens and Albertsons.

On all routes except the **Strip & Downtown Express (SDX)** fares can be paid in cash at the fare box as you enter the bus and a pass will be dispensed. Remember to have exact fare <u>as no change is given</u>!

Apart from an airport route, as a non-resident the main bus routes you will utilize, the **Strip & Downtown Express**

(SDX) and **Deuce on the Strip**, are more expensive to ride than other routes because the revenue subsidizes residential routes. Remember, the Strip transit fares do not limit your travel to the Strip, they provide access to the city's entire bus system! Current Strip & All Access fares are as follows:

• 2-Hour Strip & All Access $6 • 24-Hour Strip & All Access $8 • 3-Day Strip & All Access $20 •

TIP: Should you decide at the airport to purchase the 2 Hour Strip & All Access Pass to get to your hotel, and do not need to transfer to a Strip bus route to get there, save money by paying the residential fare at the fare box on the bus (Single Ride $2, 2-Hour Pass $3)!

♠♥♣♦

For the tourist, in addition to the airport routes, the following bus routes may be of some interest (north/south routes are numbered in the 100s and east/west routes are 200s). The two most popular routes operate on Las Vegas Boulevard:

• **Strip & Downtown Express (SDX)** operates from 9 AM to 12:30 AM.

• **Deuce on the Strip** • 24 hour service • 7 AM to 2 AM every 15 minutes; 2 AM to 7 AM every 20 minutes.

Other routes that may be of interest to the tourist include:

• **Route 212 Sunset**
Eastbound from South Strip Transfer Terminal (SSTT)

• **Route 201 Tropicana** • 24 hour service • At Las Vegas Boulevard eastbound stop is located alongside the Tropicana. Westbound stop is located next to New York-New York

• **Route 202 Flamingo** • 24 hour service • At Las Vegas Boulevard eastbound stop is located alongside Bally's. Westbound stop is located alongside Caesars Palace.

• **Sahara Express (SX)** • 24 hour service • At Las Vegas Boulevard eastbound stop is located alongside the SLS.

Deuce on the Strip
24/7 Bus Stops

Stops are serviced by the Deuce from midnight to 9 AM.
To access these stops at other times, transfer to the
Strip & Downtown Express (SDX) at Mandalay Bay

Strip & Downtown Express (SDX)

Operates 9 AM to midnight

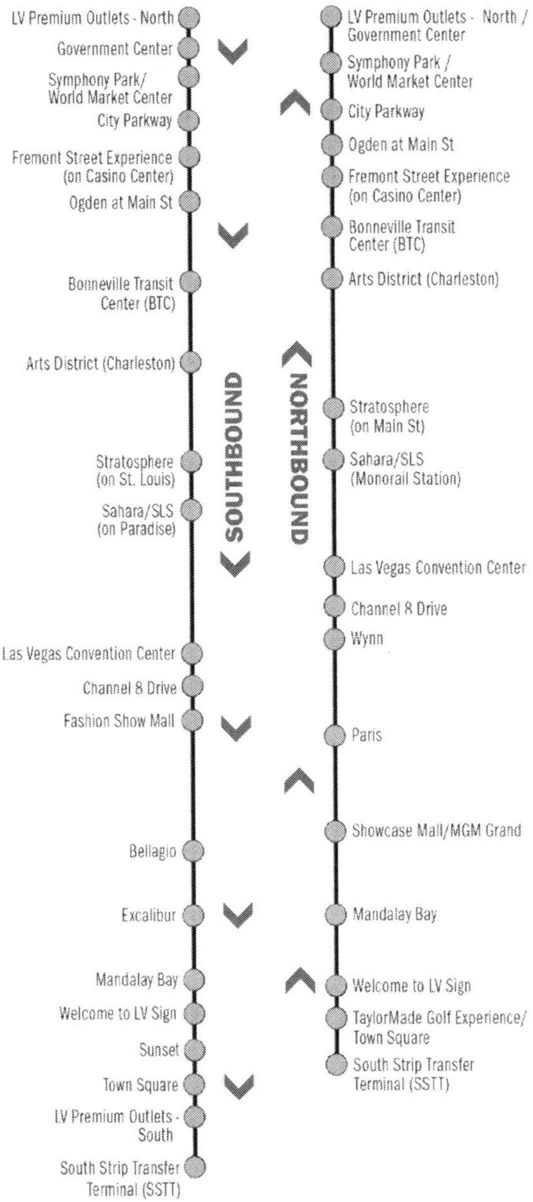
SOUTHBOUND
LV Premium Outlets - North
Government Center
Symphony Park/ World Market Center
City Parkway
Fremont Street Experience (on Casino Center)
Ogden at Main St
Bonneville Transit Center (BTC)
Arts District (Charleston)
Stratosphere (on St. Louis)
Sahara/SLS (on Paradise)
Las Vegas Convention Center
Channel 8 Drive
Fashion Show Mall
Bellagio
Excalibur
Mandalay Bay
Welcome to LV Sign
Sunset
Town Square
LV Premium Outlets - South
South Strip Transfer Terminal (SSTT)
NORTHBOUND
LV Premium Outlets - North / Government Center
Symphony Park / World Market Center
City Parkway
Ogden at Main St
Fremont Street Experience (on Casino Center)
Bonneville Transit Center (BTC)
Arts District (Charleston)
Stratosphere (on Main St)
Sahara/SLS (Monorail Station)
Las Vegas Convention Center
Channel 8 Drive
Wynn
Paris
Showcase Mall/MGM Grand
Mandalay Bay
Welcome to LV Sign
TaylorMade Golf Experience/ Town Square
South Strip Transfer Terminal (SSTT)

Westbound stops are located alongside McDonalds and World's Largest Gift Shop.

• **Boulder Highway Express (BHX)** • 24 hour service. • Southbound from Bonneville Transit Center (BTC) the first stop is on Ogden Avenue across the street from the Downtown Grand, to the left of the Downtown Grand Parking Garage entrance.

♠♥♣♦

Getting to big box discount retailers **Target** and **Walmart**, or the **Las Vegas Premium Outlets** from the Strip:

• The closest **Target** is located on East Flamingo at Maryland Parkway. Take the Flamingo 202 eastbound. A **Walmart** is further away on this same bus route at Boulder Highway. The **Walmart** stop is directly across the street from Sam's Town on Boulder Highway.

• The closest **Walmart** is on Tropicana Avenue and McLeod Drive. Take the Tropicana 201 eastbound.

• The Strip & Downtown Express (SDX) route services both **Las Vegas Premium Outlets** locations (North & South). Additionally, from Tropicana Avenue and Las Vegas Boulevard (stop alongside New York-New York) the Westcliff Airport Express (WAX) provides service to **Las Vegas Premium Outlets North**.

TIP: Nevada residents, part-year residents (see *Local Tips* chapter), tourists staying off-Strip or have no intention of utilizing the Strip bus routes, purchase the less expensive residential fare pass. Residential passes are valid system wide. Current RTC Residential fares are:

• Single Ride $2 • 2-Hour Pass $3 • 24-Hour Pass $5 •
• 15-Day Pass $34• 30-Day Pass $65 •

TIP: <u>You do not need to be a resident to obtain a reduced fare ID card</u>! Reduced Fare (50% off) Residential and Strip & All Access fares are available for youths (6-17) senior citizens over 60, persons with disabilities and Medicare eligible persons. A **Reduced Fare Identification Card** is required (available for free at Bonneville Transit Terminal).

♠♥♣♦

The Downtown Loop

The city of Las Vegas has partnered with the Regional Transportation Commission and Keolis Transit to provide a FREE shuttle service, **The Downtown Loop**. On June 27, 2017 the six-month pilot program made its inaugural run. Shuttle runs daily:

- Monday through Thursday 11:30 AM to 8:30 PM •
- Friday through Saturday 3 PM to 12 AM •
- Sunday 10 AM to 7 PM •

The Downtown Loop services stops at seven locations:
- Bonneville Transit Center – 101 E. Bonneville Avenue •
- The Arts District – Art Way and Boulder Avenue •
- Pawn Plaza – Las Vegas Blvd., South of Garces Avenue •
- Fremont East Entertainment District – Las Vegas Blvd., South of Fremont Street •
- Mob Museum – 300 Stewart Avenue •
- Fremont Street Experience – Main Street, South of Fremont Street •
- Las Vegas North Premium Outlets – South Grand Central Parkway, between Nautica and Tommy Hilfiger Kids •

RTC Bike Share

The RTC launched the valley's first public bike share system in October 2016 in Downtown Las Vegas, providing an affordable and convenient transportation choice for locals and tourists alike. The Bike Share system includes a network of 21 stations and 180 bicycles available for self-service rental 24 hours a day.

RTC Bike Share provides a convenient and easy-to-use transportation alternative to short trips in the downtown area where users can check out a bike from one station and return it to another station near their final destination. Pricing: • $4 for a 30-minute ride • $8 for a 24-hour pass • • $20 for a 30-day membership •

As part of the 24-hour pass and 30-day membership, users can check out a bike for 30 minutes at a time, for as many trips as their pass duration allows, without being charged an extra fee."

The 21 Bike Share stations are located at:
• Sahara Avenue & Las Vegas Boulevard (Walgreens) •
• Main Street & Utah Avenue •
• California Avenue & Main Street •
• 4th Street & Charleston Boulevard •
• 1st Street & Boulder Avenue (Arts District) •
• 3rd Street & Hoover Street •
• Garces Avenue & Las Vegas Boulevard •
• Bonneville Ave & Grand Central Pky (Premium Outlets) •
• Bonneville Transit Center •
• 3rd St & Bonneville Avenue •
• 11th Street & Garces Avenue •
• Maryland Parkway & Clark Avenue •
• 1st Street & Clark Avenue (City Hall) •
• 4th Street & Bridger Avenue •
• 8th Street & Bridger Avenue •
• 6th Street & Carson Avenue •
• 10th Street & Fremont Street •
• Maryland Parkway & Fremont Street •
• 8th Street & Fremont Street (Container Park) •
• Stewart Street & Las Vegas Boulevard (Zappos) •
• 3rd Street & Stewart Avenue •

Monorail System

• **Las Vegas Monorail** •
www.lvmonorail.com
• Local 702.699.8222 • Toll Free 866.466.6672 •
• Lost & Found 702.733.9069 (Mon - Fri 8 AM-5 PM) •

The east side of the Strip is serviced by a not-for-profit monorail system with seven stops. Built at a cost of around $700 million dollars, the Las Vegas Monorail opened its 3.9 mile system to the public in July 2004. The company was plagued by problems and maintenance closures, culminating with a bankruptcy filing in 2009. The company emerged from bankruptcy in 2012 with 98% of the company's debt erased, from $757 million to a more manageable $13 million!

Phase 2 of the monorail project was a 2.3 mile extension along Main Street to Downtown. The project collapsed with the failure to obtain a federal government grant. The plan for Phase 2 was revised to extend the monorail 4 miles from MGM Grand Station to both terminals at McCarran Airport. Nothing became of that plan either. Currently, a proposed 1.14 mile extension and new station between Mandalay Bay and the Luxor is traversing the permitting process. Once approved and funded, construction of the proposed extension and station could take 18 months.

Clean, fast, and convenient, the monorails electric trains provide service at seven stops. Trains arrive about every 4 to 9 minutes for the roughly 15 minute ride from end to end. To date, the monorail has served over 60 million riders!

The monorail operates seven days a week from 7 AM. On Monday it closes at 12 AM (midnight), Tuesday through Thursday it runs until 2 AM, and Friday through-Sunday until 3 AM.

Automated ticket vending machines (TVM's) are located near fare gates at each station. Customer service ticketing offices are also located near the TVM's at Bally's/Paris, Flamingo, Harrah's/LINQ, Westgate, and SLS Stations. Ticket office hours of operation are from 10 AM to 6 PM daily. The MGM Grand Station ticket office opens an hour earlier and closes an hour later (except Fri & Sat when it stays open until 9 PM).

Single ride tickets cost $5. If you plan on riding more than twice in a consecutive 24 hour period the unlimited ride passes are a better deal:

• **One-day Pass $12** (24 hour period) • **Two-day Pass $22** (48 hour period) • **Three-day Pass $28** (72 hour period) • **Four-day Pass $36** (96 hour period) • **Five-day Pass $43** (120 hour period) • **Seven-day Pass $56** (168 hour period) •

Las Vegas Monorail

North
The SLS Station

Westgate Station

Las Vegas Convention Center Station

Harrah's / The Linq Station

Flamingo / Caesars Palace Station

Bally's / Paris Station

MGM Grand Station
South

There is a 10% discount when purchasing tickets or passes online. All tickets and passes are valid for one year from purchase, and are activated upon first use at a fare gate. Children 5 and under ride free.

TIP: In the *Saving Thousands* chapter of this guide, you will find information on how to acquire unlimited ride passes on a B1G1 offer! Great deal if you're a couple traveling together, or if alone, use one now and the other on your next trip!

Discount Monorail tickets are available at all ticketing offices for locals with a valid Nevada driver's license, State of Nevada ID or Nevada Sheriff's Card. Local fare is only $1 per ride! "Maximum purchase: two single ride tickets per person per day OR one 20-ride ticket no more frequently than every ten days. Customers purchasing a 20-ride ticket may not purchase any other local tickets within the 10-day restriction time."

🚊 Free Inter-Casino Trams 🚊

Unlike the continuous Las Vegas Monorail that operates on the east side of the Strip, the west side is serviced by three separate (non-connecting) elevated trams that are free to ride!

• Mandalay Bay ↔ Luxor ↔ Excalibur Trams •

This half-mile long dual tram line links three MGM properties and operates daily from 9 AM, Sunday through Wednesday until 12:30 AM & Thursday through Saturday until 2:30 AM. The outer line is the express (Tram II) which connects Mandalay Bay and Excalibur with no stop at Luxor. The express runs approximately every 5 minutes. The inner route (Tram I) connects all three properties via Mandalay Bay. There is now no direct southbound tram between Excalibur and Luxor. At Excalibur you must board Tram II to Mandalay Bay, then transfer to Tram I for the trip back to the Luxor.

• City Center Tram •
Aria/Monte Carlo ↔ Crystals ↔ Bellagio

The newest tram service, City Center, consists of two 95-foot long trains that run simultaneously in each direction servicing three station stops. The trams travel at 13.5 miles per hour, completing the entire route in under 7 minutes. Operates from 8 AM to 4 AM daily.

• Mirage ↔ TI (Treasure Island) Tram •

Servicing the shortest route, this tram operates from 9 AM until 1 AM Sunday through Thursday, until 3 AM on Friday & Saturday. This short ride between neighboring casinos (2 to 4 minutes) departs every 15 minutes. The Mirage stop is located outside, just to the right of the hotel's main entrance. The TI stop is indoors, near the entrance to the parking garage.

Free Casino Shuttles

Except for shuttles going to and from McCarran International Airport mentioned previously, free Strip and inter-casino shuttles do not allow luggage on board. Tips are accepted, but not required. All times are approximate and subject to change. The following properties currently offer free shuttle service as listed:

• **Bally's Las Vegas** offers a complimentary shuttle to the Rio from 10 AM to 1 AM daily. Pick-up times, dependent on traffic conditions, are approximately every 30 minutes. Pick-up location is at the Race and Sports Book entrance (north entrance, on Flamingo Road).

• **California Hotel & Casino** is a stop on the Sam's Town Hotel & Gambling Hall Downtown shuttle route. Pick-up and drop-off is on First Street near valet parking. Shuttles depart the California at 8:30 AM, 9:45 AM, 11 AM, 12:15 PM, 1:30 PM, 2:45 PM, 4 PM, 5:15 PM, 6:30 PM, 7:45 PM and 9 PM.

• **Fremont Hotel & Casino** is part of the Sam's Town Hotel & Gambling Hall Downtown shuttle route. The shuttle departs from the Fremont, makes a stop at the California, continues on to Sam's Town, then makes the return trip to the Fremont. Shuttle pick-up and drop-off at the Fremont is located on Casino Center Boulevard outside the hotel lobby entrance by valet parking. Shuttles depart the Fremont at 8:15 AM, 9:30 AM, 10:45 AM, 12 PM, 1:15 PM, 2:30 PM, 3:45 PM, 5 PM, 6:15 PM, 7:30 PM and 8:45 PM.

• **Gold Coast Hotel & Casino** offers shuttle service to its sister property Orleans Hotel & Casino and then to the Strip (drops off behind the High Roller at the LINQ). The shuttle operates on a loop seven days a week, from 9 AM to 12:30 AM and picks up guests approximately every 30 minutes from the hotel's Flamingo Road entrance. Last shuttle leaves the High Roller stop at 12:30 AM. Emerald Players Club members and hotel guests receive priority seating.

• **Green Valley Ranch Resort & Spa** provides a complimentary shuttle (must be a hotel guest and present room key) departing from GVR Valet to Mandalay Bay Hotel at 12 PM, 2 PM, 4 PM and 8 PM. The shuttle picks up from Mandalay Bay at the Tour & Travel Lobby located on the lower level at 12:30 PM, 2:30 PM, 4:30 PM and 8:30 PM. For shuttle questions contact: Local 702.617.7745

• **Hard Rock Hotel & Casino** offers a complimentary shuttle service for hotel guests to and from the Fashion Show Mall. Shuttle departs the Hard Rock every hour from 10 AM until 5 PM. The return shuttle leaves the Fashion Show Mall 15 minutes after the hour.

• **Harrah's Las Vegas** offers a complimentary shuttle to the Rio from 10 AM to 1 AM daily. Pick-up times, dependent on traffic conditions, are approximately every 30 minutes. Pick-up location is at the Shuttle/Bus/Trolley drop off.

• **M Resort** provides a complimentary Strip shuttle for hotel guests to the north entrance of its sister property, the Tropicana. Shuttle departs the M at 12 PM, 2 PM, 6 PM, 10

PM and 11 PM. Shuttles from the Tropicana to the M depart 30 minutes later than the listed times.

• **Main Street Station Hotel Casino & Brewery** has no free shuttle service. However, the Sam's Town Downtown shuttle picks up across the street at a sister property, the California (connected to Main Street Station by an enclosed elevated walkway). See the California or Fremont schedule.

• **Mardi Gras Hotel & Casino** offers complimentary shuttle service to the Strip daily from 7 AM to 10 PM. For shuttle questions contact: Local 702-731-2020

• **Orleans Hotel & Casino** offers shuttle service to the Strip that drops off behind the High Roller at the LINQ and continues to its sister property Gold Coast Hotel & Casino. The shuttle operates on a loop seven days a week, from 9 AM to 12:30 AM and picks up guests approximately every 30 minutes from the hotel's Tropicana Avenue entrance. Last shuttle leaves the High Roller stop at 12:30 AM. Emerald club members and hotel guests receive priority seating.

• **Palace Station Hotel & Casino** provides a complimentary shuttle service, for hotel guests, to the Fashion Show Mall on the Strip. Shuttles depart Palace Station from 10 AM until 11 PM.

• **Palms Casino Resort** offers a shuttle service twice daily to the Fashion Show Mall at 10 AM and 5 PM. The shuttle returns to the Palms at 10:15 AM and 5:15 PM. A shuttle departs the Palms for the Forum Shops at Caesars Palace and the Fashion Show Mall at 10 AM and 5 PM. from the main valet entrance.

• **Rampart Casino/JW Marriott Las Vegas Resort** provides complimentary daily shuttle service from the Spa & Palms Towers to the north Forever 21 entrance of Fashion Show Mall on the Strip. Service is for hotel guests only. Check with the resort concierge desk for shuttle service times at: Local 702.869.7777

• **Red Rock Casino Resort & Spa** provides hotel guests complimentary shuttle service to the Fashion Show Mall on the Strip. Shuttles depart Red Rock at 11:10 AM, 1:10 PM, 3:10 PM, 5:10 PM, 7:10 PM and 9:10 PM. Shuttles return to Red Rock 30 minutes after the above posted times, with one last pick-up at 10 PM.

• **Rio Las Vegas** offers two complimentary shuttles from 10 AM to 1 AM daily. Pick-up times, dependent on traffic conditions, are approximately every 30 minutes. One shuttle runs back and forth between the Rio and Bally's, the other between the Rio and Harrah's. Pick-up location is at the Carnival World Buffet entrance.

• **Sam's Town Hotel & Gambling Hall** provides complimentary shuttle service to the Strip and Downtown from the rear casino entrance. Priority seating is given to Boyd Gaming property hotel guests (room key may be required), then B Connected members (free to join). Passengers must be 21 years of age or older, or be accompanied by someone who is.

• Sam's Town ↔ Harrah's (Strip) •

Shuttle pick-up and drop-off at Harrah's is located near valet parking at the back of the casino. The first shuttle leaves Harrah's at 9:30 AM arriving at Sam's Town at 10 AM. The first shuttle then departs Sam's Town for Harrah's at 10:10 AM. Throughout the day shuttles continue the loop on a set schedule.

Shuttles depart Sam's Town at 11 AM, 12:50 PM, 2:10 PM, 4:20 PM, 5:50 PM, 7:20 PM and 8:40 PM.

Shuttles depart Harrah's for Sam's Town at 10:50 AM, 12:10 PM, 1:30 PM, 3:40 PM, 5 PM, 6:30 PM, 8 PM and 9:10 PM.

• Sam's Town ↔ Downtown •

The Downtown shuttle stops at the Fremont and California (also Boyd Gaming properties). The first shuttle of the day departs the Fremont at 8:15 AM, makes a stop at the California (8:30 AM) and arrives at Sam's Town at 8:55 AM. Five minutes later (9 AM) the shuttle departs Sam's Town and operates in a continuous loop throughout the day.

Shuttles depart Sam's Town at 10:15 AM, 11:30 AM, 12:45 PM, 2 PM, 3:15 PM, 4:30 PM, 5:45 PM, 7 PM and 8:15 PM.

• **Silver Sevens Hotel & Casino** provides a complimentary shuttle service to the Strip at 10:30 AM, 8:30 PM, 3:30 PM and 11:30 PM.

• **Silverton Casino Hotel** provides complimentary scheduled shuttle service to and from Caesars Palace Forum Shops on the Strip, for hotel guests. Shuttles depart Silverton at 10:15 AM, 1:15 PM, 5:15 PM and 10:15 PM. The shuttle makes its return trips to Silverton 15 minutes after the times listed above.

• **Town Square Las Vegas** (a village-like shopping, dining and entertainment center) provides a complimentary shopping shuttle to and from the Hard Rock Hotel & Casino (at west hotel tower), The Tropicana (at local entrance), South Point Casino Resort (at valet) and Silverton Hotel Casino (at valet). Each shuttle guest receives a Town Square coupon book. Contact: 702 269.5001 Full shuttle schedule available at: **www.mytownsquarelasvegas.com/shuttle**

♠♥♣♦

One Strip hotel offers a **paid** shuttle service to the Strip:

• **South Point Hotel, Casino & Spa** offers a scheduled shuttle to the Strip for a **fee**. The shuttle has stops at TI (Treasure Island), City Center/Aria and the Excalibur. Shuttle operates from 8:05 AM through 1:10 AM. Tickets are purchased on board the vehicle. The cost is $8.50 round-trip per person (cash only). Current schedule available at:
www.southpointcasino.com/hotel/strip-shuttle

♠♥♣♦

LODGING

According to the Las Vegas Convention and Visitors Authority, 100% of Las Vegas visitors stay overnight paying an average rate of $120 per night. But Las Vegas offers a plethora of lodging options, ranging from motels to luxurious five star properties. However, be cautious when choosing where to stay based on advertised rates. Room rate quotes typically do not include **mandatory daily resort and parking fees**! In order to make an informed comparison of rates, be sure to read the small print on any advertised rate before booking, adding all fees to the rate quote.

Resort and parking fees are **daily** supplementary charges that **are not included in the initial booking cost**, regardless of whether you book through the hotel website or via a third party. Although the fees are due to the hotel at check-out, some hotels require payment at check-in. In return, these supplementary fees allow access to certain amenities that vary by property.

In the Las Vegas valley some properties have been charging small resort fees for many years. When low resort fees were phased in; justified by free local calls, internet, Wi-Fi, parking, etcetera; most visitors indicated that they did not pick hotels based on whether they charged a resort fee or not. However, with the advent of spiraling fees in the past few years (as high as $39 per day plus tax) consumers are beginning to take notice, especially when at times rates can be doubled after resort fees are added!

Current promotional mid-week rates of $22, $23 and $25 July through September 2017 at Circus Circus Las Vegas for example, sound like great bargains, until the resort fee of $27 per night more than doubles the rates!

♠♥♣♦

Boyd Gaming has been charging fees at some properties for many years. Station Casinos began charging resort fees in 2004. MGM Resorts added resort fees in 2008, a move initially opposed by its main competitor Harrah's Entertainment (now Caesars Entertainment). Caesars launched a "no resort fees" advertising campaign in 2010. But on March 1, 2013, Caesars embraced the resort fee. As of June 2017 resort fees on the Strip typically add $27 to $39 plus 13.38% tax <u>daily</u> to your hotel bill!

Currently, the Aztec Inn Motel & Casino and the Best Western PLUS Casino Royal are the only Strip casino/hotel properties without a resort fee. Just thirteen casino/hotel properties valley wide have resisted embracing the resort fee. Of those that have, the lowest resort fees are typically found Downtown and off-Strip. Due to the impact fees have on casino bottom lines (hundreds of millions of dollars), without self-restraint or governmental intervention resort fees are here to stay and their upward spiral will continue.

Resort fees have been a source of contention for years. As the fees are mandatory, most consumers believe that resort fees are hidden charges that should be included in the advertised room rate. How Vegas hotels advertise resort fees varies.

Kudos go to Red Rock Resorts properties for posting highlighted tax inclusive resort fees on each properties reservation page, clearly visible prior to checking dates or booking. Caesars properties require that you scroll to the bottom of the "Rate Calendar Page" in order to discover the resort fee prior to checking dates or booking. MGM Resorts properties don't display the resort fee until the "Room Choice Page." Boyd Gaming properties don't display the resort fee up-front, instead they wait until the "Guest Info Page." Even worse still, certain properties require that you must thoroughly search the website to discover resort fees and at still others, the resort fee is hidden until the final confirmation page.

One final cautionary note on resort fees … resort fees are not set on an annual basis and are adjusted at the whim and fancy of management. Most, if not all, properties increase resort fees multiple times throughout the year.

♠♥♣♦

In Nevada there is a tax imposed on room rentals of 30 days or less, which is officially known as a "transient lodging tax." In October 2016 a 0.5% room tax increase was approved by the State of Nevada and went into effect January 15, 2017. This increase will fund The Las Vegas Convention and Visitors Authority's expansion and renovation of the Convention Center. Additionally, another room tax increase of 0.5% or 0.88% (dependent on a properties location) will take effect beginning March 1, 2017. This increase is earmarked for Stadium Construction, in the hopes of attracting an NFL franchise to the Las Vegas Valley.

Dependent on a properties location, the transient lodging tax will be either 12.5%, 13% or 13.38%. Properties outside the Stadium and Priority Gaming Corridor are taxed at 12.5%. All of the Strip resorts are located within the newly created Stadium District and are taxed at the rate of 13.38%.

NOTE: Lodging tax is applied after resort fees are added to your room rate. Tax is not charged on a complimentary room night.

♠♥♣♦

Hotels in Las Vegas operate the same as hotel properties industry wide, except that a portion of rooms are blocked for casino marketing and casino players. The casino blocked rooms are available to casino hosts and those with comp authority, which includes the Pit and Slot departments. These rooms are dispersed as either a discretionary complimentary, or at a "casino rate" which is much lower than the hotels rack rate (retail). This is why rooms can sometimes be booked when a hotel appears to be sold out.

Similar to industry standards, Las Vegas hotel rack rates are established in advance based on projected occupancy levels and other factors. Rates can fluctuate drastically (normally upward) the closer you get to the arrival date, due to actual bookings increasing occupancy levels. The higher the actual occupancy level, the higher the rates.

Rack rates are updated and adjusted constantly. When you are searching for a good rate, a rate that looks good one day may not be the same the next day. The closer you get to an arrival date rates can fluctuate more often, even hourly! This occurs quite often on weekends, holidays, or during conventions and special events.

TIP: If for some reason you arrive in Las Vegas on a weekend with no room reservation, make finding lodging your first priority. Rates will probably be increasing throughout the day. Sometimes reasonable last minute rates can be found through discounters like **www.priceline.com**, **www.hotwire.com** or **www.trivago.com** .

TIP: When you come across a good hotel rate, book it, especially if a hotel cancelation policy doesn't penalize you for an advance cancelation. Should your plans change or a better deal become available, you can cancel and rebook.

TIP: For best rates book direct and online. Some properties, like MGM Resorts, now charge a fee for phone reservations.

♠♥♣♦

The following section contains hotel listings that are presented alphabetically and are by no means all-inclusive. Countless lodging only options are also available in the Las Vegas market. Each listing includes the name of the property, email; street address; local & toll free phone number; zip code; estimated taxi route mileage, time and fare from McCarran Airport,* which Regional Transportation Commission (RTC) bus routes provide service to or very near the property and **resort fee** & amenity icons.

*Taxi fare **APPROXIMATIONS** calculated utilizing the shortest route with light traffic, rounded to the nearest dollar. Estimated fares include initial meter charge, metered fare, airport fee and tax, but do not include tip or credit card surcharge. Time of day, route taken, day of week and traffic can dramatically influence the fare. No warranty, expressed or implied, is made regarding the accuracy, reliability or usefulness of this information, which is believed to be reliable. **www.taxifarefinder.com/main.php?city=LV**

♠♥♣♦

Property Amenity Codes

After each property listing there are amenity icons that represent services offered (when applicable) that may be of interest to the frugal traveler:

= Resort Fee (rounded, tax not included)

= No Resort Fee

= Parking Fees

= Complimentary Airport Shuttle

= Other Free Shuttle (Strip ● Malls ● Casinos)

= Free inter-casino tram service

= Free Wi-Fi in public areas

= Fee for use Internet Kiosk (s) available

= Movie Theater located on property

= Bitcoin ATM (Buy or Sell Bitcoins)

♠♥♣♦

Las Vegas Boulevard ("Strip")

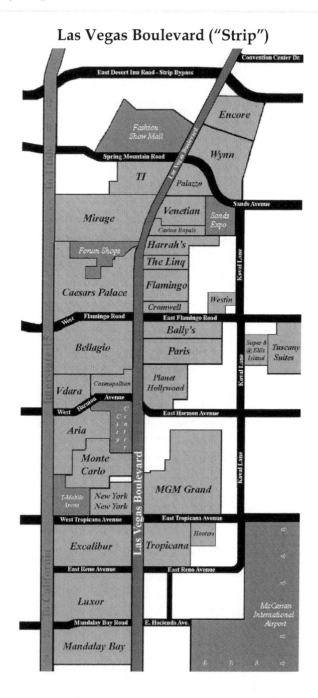

HOTELS ON THE STRIP

♠♥♣♦

• **Aria Resort & Casino** •
www.arialasvegas.com
• 3730 Las Vegas Boulevard S.• 89109 •
• Local 702.590.7111 • Toll Free 866.359.7757 •
• Airport estimate • 3.6 miles • 13 minutes • $20 •
• Strip & Downtown Express • Deuce on the Strip •

♠♥♣♦

• **Aztec Inn Motel & Casino** •
no website
• 2200 South Las Vegas Boulevard • 89104 •
• Local 702.385.4566 •
• Airport estimate • 5.6 miles • 19 minutes • $28 •
• Strip & Downtown Express • Deuce on the Strip •

♠♥♣♦

• **Bally's Las Vegas** • Formerly the MGM •
www.ballyslasvegas.com
• 3645 Las Vegas Boulevard S.• 89109 •
• Local 702.739.4111 • Toll Free 877.603.4390 •
• Airport estimate • 3.9 miles • 14 minutes • $21 •
• Strip & Downtown Express • Deuce on the Strip • 202 •

♠♥♣♦

• **Bellagio** • Built on the site of the Dunes •
www.bellagioresort.com
• 3600 Las Vegas Boulevard S.• 89109 •
• Local 702.693.7111 • Toll Free 888.987.6667 •
• Airport estimate • 4.2 miles • 15 minutes • $22 •
• Strip & Downtown Express • Deuce on the Strip • 202 •

♠♥♣♦
• Caesars Palace •
www.caesarspalace.com
• 3570 Las Vegas Boulevard S.• 89109 •
• Local 702.731.7110 • Toll Free 866.227.5938 •
• Airport estimate • 4.5 miles • 17 minutes • $24 •
• Strip & Downtown Express • Deuce on the Strip • 202 •

♠♥♣♦

• Best Western plus Casino Royale •
www.casinoroyalehotel.com
• 3411 Las Vegas Boulevard S.• 89109 •
• Local 702.737.3500 • Toll Free 800.854.7666 •
• Airport estimate • 4.3 miles • 16 minutes • $23 •
• Strip & Downtown Express • Deuce on the Strip •

♠♥♣♦

• Circus Circus Hotel & Casino •
www.circuscircus.com
• 2880 Las Vegas Boulevard S.• 89109 •
• Local 702.734.0410 • Toll Free 800.634.3450 •
• Airport estimate • 5.3 miles • 18 minutes • $26 •
• Strip & Downtown Express • Deuce on the Strip •

♠♥♣♦

• The Cosmopolitan of Las Vegas •
www.cosmopolitanlasvegas.com
• 3708 Las Vegas Boulevard S.• 89109 •
• Local 702.698.7000 • Toll Free 877.551.7778 •
• Airport estimate • 3.4 miles • 13 minutes • $20 •
• Strip & Downtown Express • Deuce on the Strip •

♠♥♣♦

• **The Cromwell of Las Vegas** •
• Formerly Barbary Coast /Bill's Gamblin' Hall & Saloon •
www.thecromwell.com
• 3595 Las Vegas Boulevard S.• 89109 •
• Local 702.777.3777 • Toll Free 844.426.2766 •
• Airport estimate • 3.9 miles • 14 minutes • $21 •
• Strip & Downtown Express • Deuce on the Strip • 202 •

♠♥♣♦

• **Encore Las Vegas** •
www.wynnlasvegas.com (combined websites)
• 3131 Las Vegas Boulevard S.• 89109 •
• Local 702.770.7800 • Toll Free 888.320.7125 •
• Airport estimate • 4.3 miles • 17 minutes • $23 •
• Strip & Downtown Express • Deuce on the Strip •

♠♥♣♦

• **Excalibur Hotel & Casino** •
www.excalibur.com
• 3850 Las Vegas Boulevard S.• 89109 •
• Local 702.597.7777 • Toll Free 800.937.7777 •
• Airport estimate • 3 miles • 9 minutes • $17 •
• Strip & Downtown Express • Deuce on the Strip •
•Westcliff Express (WAX) • 201 •

♠♥♣♦

• **Flamingo Las Vegas** •
www.flamingolasvegas.com
• 3555 Las Vegas Boulevard S.• 89109 •
• Local 702.733.3111 • Toll Free 800.732.2111 •
• Airport estimate • 4 miles • 15 minutes • $22 •
• Strip & Downtown Express • Deuce on the Strip •

♠♥♣♦

♠♥♣♦
• Harrah's Hotel & Casino •
www.harrahslasvegas.com
• 3475 Las Vegas Boulevard S.• 89109 •
• Local 702.369.5000 • Toll Free 800.214.9110 •
• Airport estimate • 4.3 miles • 16 minutes • $23 •
• Strip & Downtown Express • Deuce on the Strip •

♠♥♣♦
• The LINQ Hotel & Casino •
• Formerly the Imperial Palace and the Quad •
www.thelinq.com
• 3535 Las Vegas Boulevard S.• 89109 •
• Local 702.731.3311 • Toll Free 800.634.6441 •
• Airport estimate • 4 miles • 15 minutes • $22 •
• Strip & Downtown Express • Deuce on the Strip •

♠♥♣♦
• Luxor Hotel & Casino •
www.luxor.com
• 3900 Las Vegas Boulevard S.• 89119 •
• Local 702.262.4000 • Toll Free 877.386.4658 •
• Airport estimate • 3.9 miles • 13 minutes • $20 •
• Strip & Downtown Express • Deuce on the Strip •

♠♥♣♦
• The M Resort •
www.themresort.com
• 12300 Las Vegas Boulevard S.• 89044 •
• Local 702.797.1000 • Toll Free 877.673.7678 •
• Airport estimate • 11.3 miles • 17 minutes • $42 •
• No RTC bus service •

♠♥♣♦

♠♥♣♦
• Mandalay Bay Resort & Casino •
www.mandalaybay.com
• 3950 Las Vegas Boulevard S.• 89109 •
• Local 702.632.7777 • Toll Free 877.632.7800 •
• Airport estimate • 3.8 miles • 13 minutes • $20 •
• Strip & Downtown Express • Deuce on the Strip •

♠♥♣♦
• MGM Grand Hotel Casino • Formerly the Marina •
www.mgmgrand.com
• 3799 Las Vegas Boulevard S.• 89109 •
• Local 702.891.1111 • Toll Free 800.929.1111 •
• Airport estimate • 2.8 miles • 9 minutes • $16 •
• Strip & Downtown Express • Deuce on the Strip •
• Westcliff Express (WAX) • 201 •

♠♥♣♦
• The Mirage •
www.themirage.com
• 3400 Las Vegas Boulevard S.• 89109 •
• Local 702.791.7111 • Toll Free 800.627.6667 •
• Airport estimate • 4.4 miles • 18 minutes, $24 •
• Strip & Downtown Express • Deuce on the Strip •

♠♥♣♦
• Monte Carlo Resort & Casino •
• Being de-themed and rebranded **Park MGM** •
www.montecarlo.com
• 3770 Las Vegas Boulevard S.• 89109 •
• Local 702.730.7777 • Toll Free 800.311.8999 •
• Airport estimate • 3.4 miles • 12 minutes • $20 •
• Strip & Downtown Express • Deuce on the Strip •

• **New York-New York Hotel & Casino** •
www.nynyhotelcasino.com
• 3790 Las Vegas Boulevard S.• 89109 •
• Local 702.740.6969 • Toll Free 800.693.6763 •
• Airport estimate • 3.3 miles • 11 minutes • $19 •
• Strip & Downtown Express • Deuce on the Strip •
• Westcliff Express (WAX) • 201 •

♠♥♣♦

• **The Palazzo Hotel Casino** •
www.palazzo.com
• 3325 Las Vegas Boulevard S.• 89109 •
• Local 702.414.4100 • Toll Free 866.263.3001 •
• Airport estimate • 3.9 miles • 14 minutes • $21 •
• Strip & Downtown Express • Deuce on the Strip •

♠♥♣♦

• **Paris Casino Resort** •
www.parislasvegas.com
• 3655 Las Vegas Boulevard S.• 89109 •
• Local 702.946.7000 • Toll Free 877.796.2096 •
• Airport estimate • 3.8 miles • 16 minutes • $21 •
• Strip & Downtown Express • Deuce on the Strip •

♠♥♣♦

• **Planet Hollywood Resort & Casino** •
• Formerly the Aladdin •
www.planethollywoodresort.com
• 3667 Las Vegas Boulevard S.• 89109 •
• Local 702.785.5555 • Toll Free 866.919.7472 •
• Airport estimate • 3.5 miles • 13 minutes • $20 •
• Strip & Downtown Express • Deuce on the Strip •

♠♥♣♦

• SLS Hotel & Casino •
• Formerly the Sahara •
www.slslasvegas.com
• 2535 Las Vegas Boulevard S.• 89109 •
• Local 702.761.7000 • Toll Free 888.627.8173 •
• Airport estimate • 5.6 miles • 19 minutes • $27 •
• Strip & Downtown Express • Deuce on the Strip • SX •

♠♥♣♦

• South Point Hotel and Casino •
www.southpointcasino.com
• 9777 Las Vegas Boulevard S.• 89123 •
• Local 702.796.7111 • Toll Free 866.791.7626 •
• Airport estimate • 6.8 miles • 17 minutes • $30 •
• RTC route 117 •

♠♥♣♦

• Stratosphere Casino, Hotel & Tower •
• Formerly Bob Stupak's Vegas World •
www.stratospherehotel.com
• 2000 Las Vegas Boulevard S.• 89104 •
• Local 702.380.7777 • Toll Free 800.998.6937 •
• Airport estimate • 5.4 miles • 19 minutes • $27 •
• Strip & Downtown Express • Deuce on the Strip •

♠♥♣♦

• TI • Treasure Island Hotel & Casino •
www.treasureisland.com
• 3300 Las Vegas Boulevard S.• 89109 •
• Local 702.894.7111 • Toll Free 800.944.7444 •
• Airport estimate • 5.6 miles • 14 minutes • $26 •
• Strip & Downtown Express • Deuce on the Strip •

♠♥♣♦

♠♥♣♦

● **Tropicana Resort & Casino** ●
www.troplv.com
● 3801 Las Vegas Boulevard S.● 89109 ●
● Local 702.739.2222 ● Toll Free 888.381.8767 ●
● Airport estimate ● 2.9 miles ● 9 minutes ● $18 ●
● Strip & Downtown Express ● Deuce on the Strip ●
● Westcliff Airport Express (WAX) ● 201 ●

♠♥♣♦

● **The Venetian Resort Hotel Casino** ●
● Built on the site of the Sands ●
www.venetian.com
● 3355 Las Vegas Boulevard S.● 89109 ●
● Local 702.414.1000 ● Toll Free 866.659.9643 ●
● Airport estimate ● 4.2 miles ● 16 minutes ● $23 ●
● Strip & Downtown Express ● Deuce on the Strip ●

♠♥♣♦

● **Wynn Las Vegas** ●
● Built on the site of the Desert Inn ●
www.wynnlasvegas.com
● 3145 Las Vegas Boulevard S.● 89109 ●
● Local 702.770.7000 ● Toll Free 877.321.9966 ●
● Airport estimate ● 4 miles ● 14 minutes ● $21 ●
● Strip & Downtown Express ● Deuce on the Strip ●

♠♥♣♦

STRIP CORRIDOR HOTELS

♠♥♣♦

• Ellis Island Casino & Brewery •
www.ellisislandcasino.com
• Super 8 Motel at Ellis Island Casino •
www.super8vegas.com
• 4250 Koval Lane • 89109 •
• Local 702.794.0888 • Toll Free 800.800.8000 •
• Airport estimate • 3.1 miles • 10 minutes • $18 •
• RTC Route 202 • Just one block from the Strip •

♠♥♣♦
• Gold Coast Hotel & Casino •
www.goldcoastcasino.com
• 4000 West Flamingo Road • 89103 •
• Local 702.367.7111 • Toll Free 888.402.6278•
• Airport estimate • 5.1 miles • 15 minutes • $25 •
• RTC routes 104 • 202 •

♠♥♣♦
• Hard Rock Hotel & Casino •
www.hardrockhotel.com
• 4455 Paradise Road • 89109 •
• Local 702.693.5000 • Toll Free 800.473.7625 •
• Airport estimate • 2.3 miles • 8 minutes • $15 •
• RTC route 108 (southbound only) •

♠♥♣♦
• Hooters Casino Hotel •
• Formerly the San Remo •
www.hooterscasinohotel.com
• 115 East Tropicana Avenue • 89109 •
• Local 702.739.9000 • Toll Free 866.584.6687 •
• Airport estimate • 2.8 miles • 9 minutes • $16 •
• Westcliff Express (WAX) • 201 • Short walk to the Strip •

♠♥♣♦
- **Lucky Dragon Hotel & Casino**
  www.luckydragonlv.com
- 300 West Sahara Avenue • 89102 •
- Local 702.889.8018 • No Toll Free # •
- Airport estimate • 5.4 miles • 18 minutes • $27 •
- RTC Route SX• Short walk to the Strip •

♠♥♣♦

- **Mardi Gras Hotel & Casino** •
  www.mardigrasinn.com
- 3500 Paradise Road • 89169 •
- Local 702.731.2020 • Toll Free 800.634.6501 •
- Airport estimate • 4 miles • 12 minutes • $21 •
- RTC route 108 (southbound only) •

♠♥♣♦

- **Orleans Hotel & Casino** •
  www.orleanscasino.com
- 4500 West Tropicana Avenue • 89103 •
- Local 702.365.7111 • Toll Free 800.675.3267 •
- Airport estimate • 4.7 miles • 16 minutes • $24 •
- RTC routes 104 • 201 •

♠♥♣♦

- **Palace Station Hotel & Casino** •
  www.palacestation.sclv.com
- 2411 West Sahara Avenue • 89102
- Local 702.367.2411 • Toll Free 800.634.3101 •
- Airport estimate • 9.4 miles • 14 minutes • $36 •
- RTC routes 119 • SX •

♠♥♣♦

♠♥♣♦

● **Palms Casino Resort** ●
www.palms.com
● 4321 West Flamingo Road ● 89103 ●
● Local 702.942.7777 ● Toll Free 866.942.7770 ●
● Airport estimate ● 5.3 miles ● 16 minutes ● $26 ●
● RTC routes 104 ● 202 ●

♠♥♣♦

● **Rio All Suite Hotel & Casino** ●
www.riolasvegas.com
● 3700 West Flamingo Road ● 89103 ●
● Local 702.252.7777 ● Toll Free 866.746.7671 ●
● Airport estimate ● 5.4 miles ● 15 minutes ● $25 ●
● RTC route 202 ●

♠♥♣♦

● **Silver Sevens Hotel & Casino** ●
● Formerly the Continental / Terrible's Hotel & Casino ●
www.silversevenscasino.com
● 4100 Paradise Road ● 89156 ●
● Local 702.733.7000 ● Toll Free 800.640.9777 ●
● Airport estimate ● 2.7 miles ● 9 minutes ● $16 ●
● RTC routes 108 (southbound only) ● 202 ●

♠♥♣♦

● **Silverton Casino Hotel** ●
www.silvertoncasino.com
● 3333 Blue Diamond Road ● 89139 ●
● Local 702.263.7777 ● Toll Free 866.722.4608 ●
● Airport estimate ● 6.2 miles ● 12 minutes ● $27 ●
● RTC route 217 ●

♠♥♣♦

• Tuscany Suites & Casino •
<u>www.tuscanylv.com</u>
• 255 East Flamingo Road • 89109 •
• Local 702.893.8933 • Toll Free 877.887.2261
• Airport estimate • 3.6 miles • 12 minutes • $19 •
• RTC routes 119 • 202 •

♠♥♣♦
• Westgate Las Vegas Resort & Casino •
• Formerly the Las Vegas Hilton & LVH Hotel & Casino •
<u>www.westgateresorts.com/hotels/nevada/las-
vegas/westgate-las-vegas-resort-casino/</u>
• 3000 Paradise Road • 89109 •
• Local 702.732.5111 • Toll Free 888.796.3564 •
• Airport estimate • 4.8 miles • 16 minutes • $24 •
• RTC routes 108 • SDX •

♠♥♣♦
• Westin Las Vegas • Casino removed July 2017 •
• Formerly the Maxim Hotel & Casino •
<u>www.westinvegas.com</u>
• 160 East Flamingo Road • 89109 •
• Local 702.836.5900 • Toll Free 866.837.4215 •
• Airport estimate • 3.6 miles • 13 minutes • $20 •
• RTC route 202 • Short walk to the Strip •

♠♥♣♦
• Wild Wild West Gambling Hall & Hotel •
<u>www.daysinn.com/hotels/nevada/las-vegas/days-inn-las-
vegas-at-wild-wild-west-gambling-hall/overview</u>
• 3330 West Tropicana Avenue • 89103 •
• Local 702.740.0000 • Toll Free 800.777.1514 •
• Airport estimate • 3.8 miles • 13 minutes • $21 •
• RTC route 201 •

LOCAL AREA CASINO HOTELS

♠♥♣♦
• Aliante Casino & Hotel •
www.aliantecasinohotel.com
• 7300 Aliante Parkway • 89084 •
• Local 702.692.7777 • Toll Free 877.477.7627 •
• Airport estimate • 28.3 miles • 32 minutes • $89 •
• RTC route 119 •

♠♥♣♦
• Arizona Charlie's Boulder Casino Hotel & Suites •
www.arizonacharliesboulder.com
• 4575 Boulder Highway • 89121 •
• Local 702.951.5800 • Toll Free 888.236.9066 •
• Airport estimate • 7.3 miles • 21 minutes • $33 •
• RTC route BHX •

♠♥♣♦
• Arizona Charlie's Decatur Casino Hotel & Suites •
www.arizonacharliesdecatur.com
• 740 South Decatur Boulevard • 89107 •
• Local 702.258.5200 • Toll Free 888.236.8645
• Airport estimate • 12.2 miles • 24 minutes • $46 •
• RTC routes 103 • 207 •

♠♥♣♦
• Boulder Station Hotel & Casino •
www.boulderstation.com
• 4111 Boulder Highway • 89121 •
• Local 702.432.7777 • Toll Free 800.683.7777 •
• Airport estimate • 7.3 miles • 21 minutes • $32 •
• RTC routes 203 • BHX • SX-B •

♠♥♣♦

• Cannery Casino Hotel •
www.cannerycasino.com
• 2121 East Craig Road • 89030 •
• Local 702.507.5700 • Toll Free 866.999.4899 •
• Airport estimate • 15.5 miles • 33 minutes • $57 •
• RTC routes 219 • DVX •

♠♥♣♦

• Eastside Cannery •
www.eastsidecannery.com
• 5255 Boulder Highway • 89122 •
• Local 702.856.5300 • Toll Free 866.999.4899 •
• Airport estimate • 7.2 miles • 20 minutes • $32 •
• RTC routes 202 • BHX •

♠♥♣♦

Fiesta Henderson Casino Hotel •
• Formerly the Reserve •
www.fiestahendersonlasvegas.com
• 777 West Lake Mead Drive • 89015 •
• Local 702.558.7000 • Toll Free 888.899.7770 •
• Airport estimate • 12.7 miles • 16 minutes • $46 •
• RTC routes 217 • HDX •

♠♥♣♦

• Fiesta Rancho Station Casino Hotel •
www.fiestarancholasvegas.com
• 2400 North Rancho Drive • 89012 •
• Local 702.631.7000 • Toll Free 800.678.2846 •
• Airport estimate • 14.5 miles • 21 minutes • $52 •
• RTC routes 106 • 210 •

♠♥♣♦

• **Green Valley Ranch Resort & Spa** •
www.greenvalleyranchresort.com
• 2300 Paseo Verde Drive • 89012 •
• Local 702.617.7777 • Toll Free 866.782.9487 •
• Airport estimate • 8.2 miles • 13 minutes • $32 •
• RTC route 111•

♠♥♣♦

• **Longhorn Casino & Hotel** •
www.longhorncasinolv.com
• 5288 Boulder Highway • 89122 •
• Casino 702.435.9170 • Hotel 702.435.8888 •
• Airport estimate • 6.9 miles • 19 minutes • $30 •
• RTC routes 202 • BHX •

♠♥♣♦

• **Lucky Club Casino & Hotel** •
www.luckyclublv.com
• 3227 Civic Center Drive • 89030 •
• Local 702.399.7415 •
• Airport estimate • 13.9 miles • 31minutes • $52 •
• RTC route 218 • 110 • Requires one or more transfers •

♠♥♣♦

• **Railroad Pass Hotel & Casino** •
www.railroadpass.com
• 2800 South Boulder Highway • 89015 •
• Local 702.294.5000 • Toll Free 800.654.0877 •
• Airport estimate • 18.9 miles • 31 minutes • $65 •
• RTC route HDX • Property is located outside the city on
the way to Hoover Dam. •

♠♥♣♦
● **Rampart Casino** ●
www.rampartcasino.com
● **JW Marriott Las Vegas Resort** ●
www.theresortatsummerlin.com
● 221 North Rampart Boulevard ● 89145 ●
● Local 702.507.5900 ● Toll Free 877.869.8777 ●
● Airport estimate ● 19.3 miles ● 24 minutes ● $65 ●
● RTC routes 120 ● 209 ●

♠♥♣♦

● **Red Rock Casino, Resort & Spa** ●
www.redrocklasvegas.com
● 10973 West Charleston Boulevard ● 89135 ●
● Local 702.797.7777 ● Toll Free 866.767.7773 ●
● Airport estimate ● 17.4 miles ● 22 minutes ● $59 ●
● RTC routes 206 ● SX ●

♠♥♣♦

● **Sam's Town Hotel & Gambling Hall** ●
www.samstownlv.com
● 5111 Boulder Highway ● 89122 ●
● Local 702.456.7777 ● Toll Free 800.897.8696 ●
● Airport estimate ● 7.4 miles ● 21 minutes ● $33 ●
● RTC routes 115 ● 202 ● BHX ●

♠♥♣♦

● **Santa Fe Station Hotel & Casino** ●
www.santafestationlasvegas.com
● 4949 North Rancho Drive ● 89130 ●
● Local 702.658.4900 ● Toll Free 866.767.7771 ●
● Airport estimate ● 20.5 miles ● 31 minutes ● $69 ●
● RTC routes 101 ● 106 ● 219 ●

♠♥♣♦
• Skyline Hotel & Casino •
www.skylinehotelandcasino.com
• 1741 North Boulder Highway • 89011 •
• Hotel: 702.565.7907 • Casino 702.565.9116 •
• Airport estimate • 10.4 miles • 21 minutes • $40 •
• RTC route BHX •

♠♥♣♦
• Suncoast Hotel & Casino •
www.suncoastcasino.com
• 9090 Alta Drive • 89145 •
• Local 702.636.7111 • Toll Free 877.677.7111 •
• Airport estimate • 17 miles • 36 minutes • $61 •
• RTC routes 120 • 207 • 209 • WAX •

♠♥♣♦
• Sunset Station Hotel & Casino •
www.sunsetstation.com
• 1301 West Sunset Road • 89014 •
• Local 702.547.7777 • Toll Free 888.786.7389 •
• Airport estimate • 8.7 miles • 24 minutes • $37 •
• RTC routes 115 • 212 • 217 • HDX •

♠♥♣♦
• Texas Station Hotel & Casino •
www.texasstation.com
• 2101 Texas Star Lane • 89032 •
• Local 702.631.1000 • Toll Free 800.654.8888 •
• Airport estimate • 14.2 miles • 20 minutes • $50 •
• RTC routes 106 • 210 •

♠♥♣♦

Downtown Las Vegas

♠♥♣♦

DOWNTOWN HOTELS

All Downtown casino properties are within a few block area serviced by numerous RTC routes. The northbound routes to reach Downtown from the Strip or airport are **Deuce on the Strip**, **Strip & Downtown Express (SDX)**, **Westcliff Airport Express (WAX)** and **Centennial Express (CX)**. The closest stop to Fremont Experience and most Downtown hotels will be at Carson and 4th Street for the **WAX**, **CX** and **Deuce on the Strip**. The closest **SDX** stop is near Carson and Casino Center Boulevard. To return southbound, the circle on the Downtown map at Las Vegas Boulevard marks the location to catch the **Deuce on the Strip**. The circle on Casino Center Boulevard marks the location to catch the southbound **SDX**, **WAX** and **CX**.

RTC route **SDX** northbound has a stop directly in front of the California on Ogden Avenue and continues to Las Vegas North Premium Outlets. On its return route, the **SDX** has a stop directly across the street from the California on Ogden, and continues its route southbound to the Strip.

♠♥♣♦
• **California Hotel & Casino** •
www.thecal.com
• 12 Ogden Avenue • 89101 •
• Local 702.385.1222 • Toll Free 800.634.6505 •
• Airport estimate • 7.3 miles • 26 minutes • $34 •

♠♥♣♦
• **The D Las Vegas** •
• Formerly Fitzgerald's •
www.thed.com
• 301 Fremont Street • 89101 •
• Local 702.388.2400 • Toll Free 800.274.5825 •
• Airport estimate • 7 miles • 24 minutes • $33 •

♠♥♣♦

• **Downtown Grand Casino** •
• Formerly Lady Luck •
www.Downtowngrand.com
• 206 North 3rd Street • 89101 •
• Local 702.719.5100 • Toll Free 855.384.7263 •
• Airport estimate • 7.7 miles • 26 minutes • $35 •

♠♥♣♦

• **El Cortez Hotel & Casino** •
www.elcortezhotelcasino.com
• 600 East Fremont Street • 89101 •
• Local 702.385.5200 • Toll Free 800.634.6703 •
• Airport estimate • 7.3 miles • 24 minutes, $33 •
• Property airport shuttle is for departures only •

♠♥♣♦

• **Four Queens Hotel & Casino** •
www.fourqueens.com
• 202 Fremont Street • 89101 •
• Local 702.385.4011 • Toll Free 800.634.6045 •
• Airport estimate • 7 miles • 25 minutes • $33 •

♠♥♣♦

• **Fremont Hotel & Casino** •
www.fremontcasino.com
• 200 East Fremont Street • 89101 •
• Local 702.385.3232 • Toll Free 800.634.6460 •
• Airport estimate • 7.2 miles • 25 minutes • $33 •

♠♥♣♦

♠♥♣♦

• Golden Gate Hotel & Casino •
www.goldengatecasino.com
• One Fremont Street • 89101 •
• Local 702.385.1906 • Toll Free 800.426.1906 •
• Airport estimate • 7.2 miles • 26 minutes • $34 •

♠♥♣♦

• Golden Nugget Hotel & Casino •
www.goldennugget.com/LasVegas
• 129 East Fremont Street • 89101 •
• Local 702.385.7111 • Toll Free 844.684.4438 •
• Airport estimate • 7.7 miles • 27 minutes • $35 •

♠♥♣♦

• Main Street Station Hotel Casino & Brewery •
www.mainstreetcasino.com
• 200 North Main Street • 89101 •
• Local 702.387.1896 • Toll Free 800.713.8933 •
• Airport estimate • 9.2 miles • 25 minutes • $39 •

♠♥♣♦

• Plaza Hotel & Casino •
www.plazahotelcasino.com
• 1 Main Street • 89101 •
• Local 702.386.2110 • Toll Free 800.634.6575 •
• Airport estimate • 7.1 miles • 25 minutes • $33 •
• Property airport shuttle is for departures only •

♠♥♣♦

FRUGAL DINING

♠♥♣♦

With the opening of Wolfgang Puck's Spago restaurant in the Forum Shops at Caesars Palace in 1992, Las Vegas commenced the journey down the path to becoming a world renowned dining mecca. Many of the world's celebrity chefs; Mario Batali, Joe Bastinach, Daniel Boulud, Tom Colicchio, Scott Conant, Alain Ducasse, Todd English, Guy Fieri, Bobby Flay, Hubert Keller, Emeril Lagasse, Giada de Laurentiis, Michael Mina, Rick Moonen, Masaharu Morimoto, Wolfgang Puck, Gordon Ramsay, Joel Robuchon and Buddy Valastro; have one or more signature dining establishments in Las Vegas! On occasion, frugal dining options are even available at some of these fine establishments!

Long before the fine dining trend arrived in the valley, Vegas had a reputation for its buffets, which ranged from mediocre to extravagant! Today, overall buffet prices have increased, but a wide range of pricing and quality still exists. The mediocre appear to have remained mediocre, the average and good have increased in number, and the extravagant have excelled to even higher levels of opulence!

♠♥♣♦

One of the most successful dining fads in Vegas is all-inclusive, all-day dining. Not the bargain it was upon inception, still, a great way to spend the day indulging at numerous buffets or restaurants! But remember, if you are not prepared to eat three meals and/or snacks in a day, an all-day or 24-hour pass will not be your cheapest option.

All buffets include all-you-can-drink non-alcoholic beverages. Another Vegas fad is the all-inclusive alcoholic beverage option offered by some restaurants, buffets (MGM properties) and bars. For a set price, added to the cost of your meal, you receive unlimited alcoholic beverages!

TIP: Dependent on your specific needs and desires, in many cases it will be cheaper to utilize discount coupons instead of an all-inclusive dining option. Individual coupons also offer greater flexibility. The three main sources for the best Las Vegas coupons will be gone over in detail in the chapter *Saving Thousands*. Combined, these sources alone offer over a hundred buffet discount coupons!

Buffet of Buffets
www.caesars.com/las-vegas/buffet-of-buffets/faq
• Local 702.862.3530 •

The best all-day-buffet dining option currently available, although pricey, is the **Buffet of Buffets** offered by Caesars Entertainment (CET). The Buffet of Buffets is valid for a period of 24 hours from first use, at multiple locations. Enjoy unlimited entrance to five CET property buffets; two more buffet options are available with a ***per visit up-charge**.

• Regular price is $59.99 plus tax Sunday ↔ Thursday •
• $74.99 plus tax Weekends & Holidays •

For this promotion a weekend is considered to be from 11 AM Friday ↔ 11 AM Sunday. There are no Total Rewards Players Club discounts on Buffet of Buffets pricing.

In order to ascertain the cost of all available options, the following listings include promotional and regular pricing information. All buffets include non-alcoholic beverages and gratuity is not included. Passes that expire while customer is in line, will be considered expired upon reaching cashier! Blackout dates may apply, including holidays, convention periods and special events. The Buffet of Buffets cannot be used in conjunction with any other offer or promotion (no coupons). Additional restrictions may apply. Valid only at the following Caesars Entertainment venues:

• **Paradise Garden Buffet at the Flamingo** •
www.caesars.com/flamingo-las-vegas/restaurants/paradise-garden-buffet
• Local 702.733.3111 •

Regular pricing and hours:
- Brunch ● $21.99 ● Monday ↔ Friday ● 7 AM ↔ 2 PM ●
- Brunch ● $24.99 ● Saturday & Sunday ● 7 AM ↔ 2 PM ●
- Dinner ● $29.99 ● Friday & Saturday ● 5 PM ↔ 10 PM ●

♠♥♣♦
● Flavors at Harrah's Las Vegas ●
www.caesars.com/harrahs-las-vegas/restaurants/flavors-the-buffet
● Local 702.369.5000 ●

Regular pricing and hours:
- Breakfast ● $19.99 ● Monday ↔ Friday ● 7 AM ↔ 11 AM ●
- Lunch ● $23.99 ● Monday ↔ Friday ● 11 AM ↔ 4 PM ●
- Dinner ● $29.99 ● Monday ↔ Friday ● 4 PM ↔ 9:30 PM ●
- Dinner ● $32.99 ● Saturday & Sunday ● 4 PM ↔ 9:30 PM ●
- Brunch ● $26.99 ● Saturday & Sunday ● 7 AM ↔ 4 PM ●

♠♥♣♦
● Spice Market Buffet at Planet Hollywood ●
www.caesars.com/planet-hollywood/restaurants/spice-market-buffet
● Local 702.785.5555 ●

Regular pricing and hours:
- Breakfast ● $21.99 ● Monday ↔ Friday ● 7 AM ↔ 11 AM ●
- Lunch ● $24.99 ● Monday ↔ Friday ● 11 AM ↔ 3 PM ●
- Dinner ● $30.99 ● Monday ↔ Friday ● 3 PM ↔ 11 PM ●
- Dinner ● $33.99 ● Saturday & Sunday ● 3 PM ↔ 11 PM ●
- Brunch ● $30.99 ● Sat & Sun ● 10 AM↔3 PM●

♠♥♣♦
● Le Village Buffet at Paris Las Vegas ●
www.caesars.com/paris-las-vegas/restaurants/le-village-buffet
● Local 702.946.7000 ●

Regular pricing and hours:
- Breakfast ● $21.99 ● Weekdays ● 7 AM ↔ 11 AM ●
- Breakfast ● $23.99 ● Weekends ● 7 AM ↔ 10 AM ●
- Lunch ● $24.99 ● Monday ↔ Friday ● 11 AM ↔ 3 PM ●
- Dinner ● $30.99 ● Weekdays ● 3 PM ↔ 10 PM ●
- Dinner ● $30.99 ● Weekends ● 3 PM ↔ 11 PM ●
- Brunch ● $30.99 ● Saturday & Sunday ● 10 AM ↔ 3 PM ●

♠♥♣♦
• Carnival World & Seafood Buffet at the Rio •
www.caesars.com/rio-las-vegas/restaurants/carnival-world-
buffet-and-seafood-buffet
• Local 702.777.7757 •

Regular pricing and hours:
• Dinner • $32.99 • Mon ↔ Thu • 4 PM ↔ 10 PM •
• Dinner • $34.99 • Fri, Sat, Sun • 3 PM ↔ 10 PM •
• Brunch • $31.99 • Saturday & Sunday • 10 AM ↔ 3 PM •

The **Village Seafood Buffet** is inside the Carnival World Buffet and operates for dinner only. Seafood upgrade is $20.
*Buffet of Buffets additional up-charge per visit, $25.
♠♥♣♦
• Bacchanal Buffet at Caesars Palace •
www.caesars.com/caesars-palace/restaurants/bacchanal-
buffet
• Local 702.731.7928 •

Regular pricing and hours:
• Weekday Brunch • $39.99 • Mon ↔ Fri • 7:30 AM↔3PM•
• Weekend Brunch • $49.99 • Sat & Sun • 8 AM ↔ 3 PM •
• Dinner • $54.99 • Mon ↔ Thu • 3 PM ↔ 10 PM •
• Dinner • $57.99 • Fri, Sat, Sun • 3 PM ↔ 10 PM •
*Buffet of Buffets additional up-charge per visit: $25 for Brunch or $35 for Dinner.

Because this pass is valid for unlimited buffet entry at participating locations for 24 hours from the time of initial purchase, simple planning can stretch this promotion over a two day period! By so doing, you can eat like a king in Las Vegas for as low as $30 per day!

In order to get the greatest value out of this promotion under normal conditions, you would need to enjoy four meals. Dependent upon time of purchase, you can enjoy either; two breakfasts & one lunch & one dinner; two lunches & one dinner & one breakfast; or two dinners & one breakfast & one lunch. To attain the greatest value for your money, purchase your pass at a dinner buffet and plan to eat dinner the next evening prior to the passes expiration! If you limit your dining to the more expensive buffets (but not the up-charge buffets) your savings will be greater. Of course, you could eat lighter snacks and visit every buffet!

♠♥♣♦

There are a few Vegas buffet venues that are attempting to cash-in on the Buffet of Buffets' success by offering all-day dining options of their own. However, unlike the Buffet of Buffets, these are not 24 hour dining passes. Instead, these are an all-day pass, based on a calendar day. If you utilize this option, to attain the best value for your money purchase a pass in the morning to enjoy three or more meals/snacks.

MGM Resorts International's Take 2 Pass

The Luxor **MORE Buffet** & **The Buffet** at Excalibur have brought back the **TAKE 2 PASS,** get "Both Buffets One Great Price!" Passes can be purchased from the cashier at either buffet.

All-day-buffet pricing: (subject to change during holidays)
• $39.99 • Monday ↔ Thursday • 7 AM ↔ 10 PM •
• $44.99 • Friday ↔ Sunday • 7 AM ↔ 10 PM •

♠♥♣♦

• Luxor all-day buffet option •
www.luxor.com/en/restaurants/more-the-buffet-at-luxor.html
• Local 702.262.4000 •

Regular pricing and hours:
• Breakfast • $17.99 • Monday ↔ Friday • 7 AM ↔ 11 AM •
• Lunch • $18.99 • Monday ↔ Friday • 11 AM ↔ 4 PM •
• Dinner • $23.99 • Daily • 4 PM ↔ 10 PM •
• Steak Night Dinner • $26.99 • Fri & Sat • 4 PM ↔ 10 PM •
• Weekend Brunch • $21.99 • Sat & Sun • 7 AM ↔ 4 PM •

♠♥♣♦

• Excalibur all-day-buffet option •
www.excalibur.com/en/restaurants/the-buffet.html
• Local 702.597.7446 •

Regular pricing and hours:
- Breakfast • $18.99 • Monday ↔ Friday • 7 AM ↔ 11 AM •
- Lunch • $19.99 • Monday ↔ Friday • 11 AM ↔ 4 PM •
- Dinner • $24.99 • Monday ↔ Thursday • 4 PM ↔ 10 PM •
- Dinner • $27.99 • Friday ↔ Sunday • 3 PM ↔ 10 PM •
- Brunch • $22.99 • Saturday & Sunday • 7 AM ↔ 3 PM •
- **Lunch Mon ↔ Fri w/unlimited draft beer & wine** •

♠♥♣♦

Boyd Gaming All-Day Buffet Dining

The **French Market Buffet** at The Orleans and **Ports O' Call Buffet** at Gold Coast offer all-day-dining options. Valid at both buffets, passes can be purchased from the cashier at either buffet. **TEMPORARILY DISCONTINUED PENDING DURING ORLEANS BUFFET REMODELING**

♠♥♣♦

• Orleans Hotel & Casino •
www.orleanscasino.com/dine/french-market-buffet
• Local 702.365.7111 •

During remodeling reduced hours:
- Breakfast • $11.99 • Everyday • 8 AM ↔ 2 PM •
- Lunch • $11.99 • Everyday • 11 AM ↔ 2 PM •

♠♥♣♦

• Gold Coast Hotel & Casino •
www.goldcoastcasino.com/dine/ports-o-call-buffet
• Local 702.367.7111 •

Regular pricing and hours:
- Breakfast • $8.99 • Mon ↔ Saturday • 7 AM ↔ 10 AM •
- Lunch • $10.99 • Monday ↔ Saturday • 11 AM ↔ 3 PM •
- Dinner • $15.99 • Saturday ↔ Thursday • 4 PM ↔ 9 PM •
- Seafood Dinner • $22.99 • Friday • 4 PM ↔ 9 PM •
- Champagne Brunch • $15.99 • Sunday • 8 AM ↔ 3 PM •

♠♥♣♦

TIP: Dependent on your B Connected Players Club status, the Orleans and Gold Coast buffets offer a discount off regular buffet pricing, but not on the all-day option. Ruby members get $1 off, Sapphire members get $3 off and

Emerald members get $5 off! Combine your Players Club discount with a coupon for even greater savings!

♠♥♣♦

Prepaid Dining Vouchers

There are numerous nationwide <u>online</u> sources for discounted, pre-paid dining vouchers to restaurants in Las Vegas. Some offer a sign-up bonus to new members, run sales and/or use promotional codes. These companies also offer pre-paid vouchers for attractions, shows, lounges, clubs and hotel accommodations. Participating merchants and offers are constantly being updated.

• Living Social •
www.livingsocial.com/cities/30-las-vegas
• <u>NOT</u> Toll Free 202.400.2100 •

Living Social has a sign-up offer, $10 toward purchase of $20 or more. A recent search shows dining offers available for • **Carlos'n Charlie's** • **Señor Frog's** • **Pampas Brazilian Grille** • **Bertolucci Brazilian Steakhouse** • **Bacon Boys** • **Gyu-Kaku Japanese BBQ** • **Crab Catcher** • There is a much larger inventory of attraction, show, lounge and club offers.

• Groupon •
www.groupon.com/local/las-vegas
• Toll Free 888.664.4482 •

Groupon has a sign-up offer, typically $10 toward a single purchase of $25 or more or 25% off. A recent search shows a wider dining selection at Groupon than Living Social, including • **Spice Market Buffet** • **Señor Frog's** • **Pampas Brazilian Grille** • **Vince Neil's Tatuado** • **Envy Steakhouse** • **Famous Daves BBQ** • **Primeburger** • **Hexx** • **Café 6 at Palms** • **Waffle Bar** • **Rainforest Café** • **House of Blues** • **Crab Corner** • **SEA** • **McFadden's** • Groupon's inventory also contains a wide selection of offers for hotel accommodations, attractions, shows, lounges and clubs.

• Travel Zoo •
https://www.travelzoo.com/local-deals/Las-Vegas/deals/
• Toll Free 877.665.0000 •

Functioning similar to Living Social and Groupon, travel sites like **Travel Zoo** can be a good source for prepaid discount dining, show and attraction certificates to use while in Vegas. A recent search shows 13 Las Vegas dining offers available, including • **Spice Market Buffet** • **Pampas Brazilian Grille** • **Margaritaville** • **BLT Steak** • **Edge Steakhouse** • **SEA** • **Guy Savoy** • **Hash House-A-Go-Go** •

• Viator •
https://www.viator.com/Las-Vegas/d684-ttd
• Toll Free 866. 648.5873 •

Viator is a third party international travel tour and activity company. The Viator website advertises 10% off your first purchase and a Low Price Guarantee. Viator offers a wide selection of prepaid dining and beverage tours in Las Vegas. A recent search reveals offers for • **Downtown Food Tour** • **Strip Afternoon Food Tour** • **Strip Evening Food Tour** • **Happy Hour at the LINQ** •**Boozy Brunch Tour** • **Bar & Nightclub Crawl** • **Tasting at the Whiskey Attic** • **Party Bus Hop** • **Brewery Tours** • **Nightclub Tour** •

The site had but one prepaid dining offer, the **Hard Rock Café**. Offerings and venues are subject to change. Viator also has a wide selection of show and attraction offerings.

• The Radio Shopping Show^{sm} •
www.kshp.com
• Local 702.221.1200 •

The **Radio Shopping Show** is a barter marketing program where businesses offer products and services on the radio show in exchange for advertising and publicity. Vouchers are sold at a discount off face value to members. Membership is free, sign-up online for a free Money Saver Key Tag (membership card), which will be mailed to you.

This program offers various ways to save. During the radio broadcasts (KSHP AM 1400) listeners call in and obtain 40 to 60% (or more) savings on travel destinations, fast food, family or fine dining, entertainment, weekend getaways, recreation, and other items. But you do not need to listen and call in to benefit from the program! You can visit one of the "Road Shows" at various locations throughout the Vegas area on certain dates (advertised on the radio and posted on the website) to purchase vouchers. You can also shop online 24 hours a day. Purchased vouchers can be picked up at the Redemption Center on 2400 S. Jones Boulevard #3 during business hours, at a "road show" or they can be mailed.

Program participants include restaurants, home & office retailers, personal care and automotive services. Voucher inventory is in constant flux and currently appears rather sparse on Strip area dining, but options still include: ● **Waffle Bar @Bally's** ($10 voucher for $5) ● **Strip Bar & Grill** ($25 for $12) ● **Hash House–A-Go-Go** ($25 for $12) ● **Treasure's Gentlemen's Club & Steakhouse** ($40 for $18) ● **Pampas Brazilian Grille** ($100 for $49) ● **Harbor Palace Seafood Restaurant** ($10 for $4) ●

There is always a good selection of attraction, entertainment and show vouchers available through the program! Currently there are 19 show voucher options available!

Four times a year the program has a 24 hour "Marathon Radio Shopping Show" featuring overstocked vouchers and an array of items over and above their extensive inventory. All are sale priced for greater savings than normal!

♠♥♣♦

Discount Cards & Coupon Programs

When management decides to market through coupon and discount programs, their venue will generally have offers available through numerous different vendors. Once you have determined which venues you plan to patronize in Vegas, compare all venue specific options and programs to attain the greatest savings!

TIP: It must be stated that in many cases cheaper options may be available to the frugal traveler. The three best options are described in the *Saving Thousands* chapter.

Coupons and discount cards typically provide a set percentage off (10-50%) or a B1G1 offer at each venue. The following discount and coupon offerings are not free, they must be purchased.

• Las Vegas Bite Card•
www.vegasbitecard.com
• Online contact only •

The **Las Vegas Bite Card** will get you savings on Vegas shows, tours, attractions, restaurants, nightclubs, golf and spas. Simply show your card at participating merchants to receive a discount. Discounts range from 10% to 50% off. Costs $34.95 and provides unlimited use for one year. Some dining venues include:

• **Hard Rock Café** • **Cabo Wabo Cantina** • **Hash House-A-Go-Go** • **Hofbrauhaus Las Vegas** • **Maggiano's Little Italy** • **Pampas Brazilian Grille** • **Johnny Rockets** • **New York Pretzel** • **Nathan's** • **Bonnanno's New York Pizzeria** • **Nestle Toll House Café** • **Fat Burger** • **Häagen Dazs** • **Pan Asian Express** • **Original Chicken Tender** • **L.A. Subs** •

♠♥♣♦
• VIP Dine 4Less•
www.dine4lesscard.com/?location=Las+Vegas
• Online contact only •

The **VIP Dine 4Less** typical discount is 20% off entire check or 20% off food portion only. Cost is $29.99 and discount is good for up to four adults dining together. Card is valid for 90 days.

• **Andre's** • **Bella Panini** • **Blue Martini** (50%) • **Border Grill** • **Bonnanno's New York Pizzeria** • **Cabo Wabo Cantina** • **Charlie Palmer Steak** •**Häagen Dazs** • **Hash House-A-Go-Go** (25%) • **La Salsa Cantina** • **Pampas Brazilian Grille** • **Johnny Rockets** • **New York Pretzel** • **Nathan's** • **Tacos n' Ritas** • **L.A. Subs** • **Pan Asian Express** • **Original Chicken Tender** • **Tamba** (25%) •

♠♥♣♦
• Shop & Dine Las Vegas Privilege Card•
www.shopanddinelasvegas.com/
• Local 702.369.8382 •

The **Shop & Dine Las Vegas Privilege Card** package sells for $40.00 and is valid for two people. In addition to mall dining venues, hundreds of shopping offers are available at: • **Forum Shops** • **Fashion Show** • **Grand Canal Shoppes** • **Las Vegas Premium Outlets (North & South)** • **Miracle Mile Shops** • **Macy's** • **Kay Jewelers** • **Town Square** •

CAUTION: This "package" consists of mall/outlet coupon booklets ("Passports") which are typically available for free. Some Passport booklets may require that you provide a coupon, but coupons can easily be found within free tourist publications or online. Check the *Saving Thousands* chapter for more information on mall/outlet coupon sources.

♠♥♣♦
• Las Vegas Perks •
www.lasvegasperks.com
• Local 702.616.4052 •

Another discount dining option, the **Las Vegas Perks Discount Package**, advertises over $1,500 in savings through offers for dining, shows, tours and attractions. Las Vegas Perks is a mobile smart phone package. Offers are redeemable on Mobile Smart Phones. No App, download or printing required.

Most offers are B1G1 (one offer is good for two people), but work for 50% off if dining alone. All offers are one-time use and are valid for six months from date of purchase, unless a show or venue closes. The package costs $25 and currently contains nine Food & Beverage offers:

• **Le Village Buffet** @ Paris • B1G1 or 50% off •
• **Silver Sevens Buffet** @ Silver Sevens • B1G1 or 50% off •
• **Spice Market Buffet** • Planet Hollywood • 30% discount•
• **Pampas Brazilian Grille** @ Planet Hollywood • B1G1 entrée (up to $25) or 50% off if dining alone •

- **Pampas Brazilian Grille** @ Planet Hollywood • B1G1 lunch or dinner RODIZIO (up to $52) or 50% off •
- **The Sterling Spoon Café** @ Silver Sevens • B1G1 entrée or 50% off if dining alone •
- **The Tilted Kilt Restaurant** @ the LINQ • 25% off •
- **Carlos'n Charlies** @ Flamingo • B1G1 appetizer to $14 •
- **Rainforest Café** (near Planet Hollywood) • purchase an entrée, get a free appetizer up to $14 •
- **Señor Frog's** @ TI • Open bar for one person from 9 PM until last call. Coupon is good for a $20 discount off the regular price of $45. Valid Sunday ↔ Thursday •

• Tix4Dinner •
www.tix4tonight.com/las-vegas-restaurant-coupons/
• Toll Free 877.849.4868 •

Tix4Tonight (listed in *Entertainment Values* chapter) is probably the number one source for discount same day show tickets in Vegas. This company's Tix4Dinner service also sells discount dining coupons to numerous Las Vegas restaurants. Discounts range from 50% off an entrée to 25-50% off your entire dining check (excluding alcohol). This is a good source for discount coupons valid at celebrity chef restaurants!

Discount dining coupons cost $3 per person and are sold out of **Tix4Tonight's** booths on the Strip and Downtown • **Grand Bazaar Shops** @ **Bally's** • **Planet Hollywood** • **Showcase Mall** • **Giant Coke Bottle** @ **Showcase Mall** • **Casino Royale** • **Fashion Show Mall** • **Circus Circus** • **Slots of Fun** • **Four Queens** • **Town Square Mall** •

• Restaurant.com •
www.restaurant.com/city-cuisine/lasvegas-restaurants
• Toll Free 855.832.8728 •

If you have not heard of **Restaurant.com**, now would be a great time to sign-up for this nationwide online dining program, to save on dining in Vegas and at home! A $10 credit is offered at sign-up to try the program.

The company sells discounted dining certificates to Las Vegas area restaurants and thousands more nationwide! There is absolutely no cost to set up an account and no minimum purchase requirements. Your online or mobile account keeps track of certificates purchased until redeemed and provides easy access to print unused certificates.

Restaurant specific gift certificates, depending on which denominations are offered by each specific restaurant location, are sold at 40% of face value ($100 costs $40) in increments of $5, $10, $15, $25, $50, $75 and $100. Savings are even greater during the company's frequent sales.

Once you have opened an account you will receive emails advertising sales and promotions, typically a discount code that you apply against your purchase. A recent code amounted to a 60% discount off an entire order. Therefore, a $100 gift certificate cost only $16! Sales typically range from 40-90% off, so stock up when certificates are cheapest! Don't have a discount code? An online search for "restaurant.com discount code" should provide a current code.

Gift Certificate terms and conditions for each specific restaurant are clearly spelled out online prior to purchase, and are set in stone upon purchase. Typically, the certificates are for dine in only; limited to one per party, per month, per restaurant; and all certificates require additional consideration paid to the restaurant. For example, the current $25 Certificate for **Señor Frog's** requires a minimum purchase of $50 and the $50 Certificate requires a minimum purchase of $100.

A great benefit to this program is that almost all of the participating restaurants have menus posted for your viewing before, during, or after your purchase! Once you purchase a gift certificate you either display it to the restaurant on your mobile device or print it out for immediate or future use, certificates do not expire! If an unused restaurant certificate you've purchased is not accepted by the issuer, or the restaurant goes out of business, the certificate will be replaced online free of charge!

Currently, the Strip area inventory of restaurant certificates is not as extensive as in the past. A recent search listed • **Carlos'n Charlie's** • **Señor Frog's** • **Pampas Brazilian Grille** • **Hussong's Cantina** • **House of Blues** • **Spike Market Buffet** • **Harbor Palace Seafood Restaurant** •

Certificate inventory changes constantly. A recent search showed over 180 participating restaurants within a 10 mile radius of the Strip! Certificates can sell out, but are restocked monthly. New venues are constantly being added.

♠♥♣♦

• 2017 Las Vegas Entertainment® Book •
www.shop.entertainment.com/products/las-vegas-coupon-book

Another good source for hundreds of discount coupons for the Las Vegas valley is an annual **Entertainment Membership**. Available nationwide, the $35 membership fee includes an *Entertainment® Book* loaded with hundreds of B1G1 and up to 50% off coupon discounts on fine & casual dining, fast food & carryout, activities, attractions, movie tickets, retail, services, hotels, car rentals, airlines and more for the city of your choice. The cost of the book/membership goes down the later it gets in the year (typically as low as half-price by the middle of the year). Coupons are valid through December 30, 2017.

Coupons are geared mainly to local area establishments. However, some casino and Strip area restaurants still provide the tourist with many discount dining options including • **Rainforest Café** • **Planet Hollywood** • **Crab Corner** • **Hennessey's Tavern** • **T.G.I Fridays** • **Margaritaville** • **Pampas Brazilian Grille** • **India Masala** •

TIP: In addition to printed form, the *2017 Las Vegas Entertainment® Book* is available as a digital membership instead (online and mobile app). The cost for this service is $1.99 per month (first month trial is only 99¢) or $19.99 per year. No minimum commitment, cancel anytime.

♠♥♣♦

Casino Dining Promotions

For the frugal traveler, it could be said that the best meal is the free meal! But it is possible that even though free, a meal can be disappointing or mediocre. However, the same holds true for an expensive meal, sometimes quality doesn't live up to our expectations. For me it is the self-satisfaction, that feeling of accomplishment which makes you feel special and rewarded, that makes a free meal much more appetizing and enjoyable!

For the gambler, some of the best casino promotions are structured around free or discounted buffets. Even with minimal play, you can score great buffet deals. Please refer to the chapter *Frugal Gaming* for more information on Players Clubs and how to take advantage of these programs. When visiting casinos, be on the lookout for posters advertising any current promotions. Currently, Boyd Gaming has some of the best gaming/dining/senior promotions in the valley!

Whether a tourist or local, if you are over 50 take advantage of Boyd Gaming's **Young At Heart** promotion at the Orleans, Gold Coast, Suncoast and Sam's Town every Wednesday! Once you've enrolled your Players Card in the promotion, swipe your card at any kiosk and receive a mystery point multiplier of up to 50X points! When you earn 10 base points you receive a B1G1 buffet voucher. Earn 50 base points and receive a free Breakfast or Lunch buffet. Earn 100 base points for a free Dinner buffet. You only need to earn 100 points to get all three offers! Promotional buffet vouchers are only valid on the day of issue and at the property where they were earned. Vouchers can be earned and redeemed at one, or all four properties!

A separate but similar **Young At Heart** promotion runs every Wednesday at Boyd Gaming's Downtown properties; the Fremont, California and Main Street Station. However, to participate in the promotion at the California and Main Street Station, you must be local residents with an 890** or

891** zip code. The California's promotional buffet vouchers are valid at Main Street Station's Garden Court Buffet.

♠♥♣♦

Restaurant and Café Promotions

Sometimes overlooked by visitors, national restaurant chain loyalty programs are quite prevalent in Vegas. Some even offer a new member sign-up bonus, typically a free menu item, appetizer or desert with purchase.

Save by purchasing restaurant chain gift vouchers or cards in advance through online discounters **www.cardpool.com** **www.giftcardgranny.com** or **www.raise.com.** Raise.com for example, currently has a plethora of offerings that include **Buca di Beppo** (22% off), **Hooters** (12% off), **Claim Jumper** (5% off), **Hard Rock Café** (5% off), **Rainforest Café** (6.2% off) and **Texas de Brazil** (11% off). Raise offers a $10 sign-up bonus off your first purchase of $25 or more!

TIP: Costco is a great source for Vegas area dining gift cards (bundled in $100 increments), which are typically sold for at least 20% off face value! The best selection is online and you do not need to be a member to shop online (5% surcharge)! Current gift card offerings include ● **Buca di Beppo** ● **Texas de Brazil** ● **Coldstone** ● **PF Chang's** ● **California Kitchen** ● http://www.costco.com/cash-cards-gift-certificates.html?refine=263110+

TIP: Use a discounted restaurant gift card in combination with a loyalty reward or coupon for even greater savings!

♠♥♣♦

Other great low cost dining options for the frugal minded traveler are casino café/restaurant promotions and specials. However, specials are not always advertised, so ask the hostess or your server before ordering. As can be seen in the chapter *Saving Thousands*, some casino cafés offer coupons that can stretch your budget even further!

Probably the best Vegas off-menu Steak Special is served 24 hours a day at the **Ellis Island Café**. You get a filet-cut top sirloin with soup of the day or salad, a choice of potato and green beans for $12.99! Two discount coupons can be obtained from a Players Club kiosk to lower the cost even more! All Players Club members can swipe for a daily coupon to get the Steak Special for only $9.99 (good for up to four people)! After playing $5 of coin-in on any Slot or Video Poker machine, a kiosk swipe will get a coupon for another $2 off, bringing the price down to $7.99 (one required per person)! The café also offers daily specials and a King Cut Prime Rib Dinner for $14.99!

The **Ellis Island Micro Brewery** makes the best root beer in the state! **Metro Pizza** located inside Ellis Island runs two great specials: get 2 for 1 large Pizzas on Sundays and 2 for 1 slices or whole pizzas on Thursdays!

Another good off-menu steak special is available 24 hours a day at **Mr. Lucky's** at the Hard Rock Hotel & Casino. The $7.77 Gambler's Special (w/Players Card) includes a steak, three grilled shrimp and mashed potatoes.

A little known gem, the **Market Street Café** at the California, offers three daily specials. Choose from the "Chef's Catch of the Day" or two other options, served from 11 AM to 11 PM for only $8.99! An 8 oz. cut Prime Rib Dinner Special for $9.99 is served with soup or salad, vegetable, choice of starch and cherries jubilee ice cream. Pay for your meals with Players Club points and receive 40% off!

The sole **Tony Roma's** location in Vegas (Downtown at the Fremont) offers two extremely popular specials served with a baked potato and house vegetable. From 4:30 PM to 6:30 PM you can get a Prime Rib Dinner for $8.99! From 9 PM to 11 PM the Steak & Lobster Tail Dinner is $11.99!

Another Boyd Gaming establishment, the **Courtyard Café** at the Orleans, offers a pricier "Players Choice 24-Hour Special." Served with a house salad, baked potato or fries, a 16 ounce T-Bone Steak with fried onion rings for $16.99.

If you weigh over 350 pounds, you can get a free Single Bypass Burger & Fries with the purchase of a drink at the **Heart Attack Grill** located on the east end of Fremont Street

Experience in the Neonopolis building! Offer is unlimited, but you must order one at a time.

TIP: Downtown parking. The Fremont Street Experience parking garage is located at 111 S. 4th Street. Rates are $2 per hour, $12 maximum. City owned parking is also available under the Neonopolis building, also located on 4th Street just after the Fremont Street Experience parking garage. Parking is free at the Neonopolis for the first hour and only $1 per hour thereafter with a maximum charge of $5! To access either parking garage stay in the far right hand lane on 4th Street (4th Street is one-way traffic only).

♠♥♣♦

If you're serious about eating challenges, Vegas area restaurants will not disappoint. Check out some of these food & beverage options, although many other offers are available! Start things off with a few beers . . .

Todd English P.U.B. (The Shops at Crystals) has the Seven-Second Beer Challenge. "Slam a Beer (pint) in 7 seconds or less and it's on the house!" Certain restrictions apply.

PBR Rock Bar (Miracle Mile Shops) has the PBR Challenge, a two pound burger with a half-pound each of Cheddar cheese, hot dogs and chili, topped with four fried pickles. The burger is served with a pound of fries and a 24-ounce milkshake for $48. Finish everything within 30 minutes and it's FREE, you also get a T-Shirt and $50 in PBR Bucks!

Toby Keith's I Love This Bar & Grill (Harrah's) has the Big Dog Daddy 100 Ounce Challenge. A two pound Angus burger served on a 10 oz. bun with 4 oz. each of cheese, lettuce, tomato and onion, 2 oz. dill pickle spear, pound of seasoned fries, 32 oz. Coors Light and southern fried Twinkies. Complete this challenge and get a free t-shirt.

Cheeseburger Las Vegas (Miracle Mile Shops) has the Cheeseburger Challenge. Three burger patties, Swiss & Colby Jack cheese, Thousand Island dressing, mayonnaise, sautéed onions, fried egg, bacon, Kalua pork, sautéed mushrooms, jalapeños, lettuce, tomato and pickles on a salt & pepper bun served with a pile of chili cheese fries and topped with onion rings. Finish the whole thing in 20 minutes or less and it is free!

Diablo's Cantina (Monte Carlo) has the Death Wing Challenge. Chicken wings tossed in hot sauces. "We start with Anaheims, move up to Fresno's then the Jalapeños, your eyes start watering with the Serrano's, only to have the Scotch Bonnet's as a dessert." Those who cannot complete the challenge make the wall of shame, eat it all and make the wall of fame and get a free t-shirt.

Rockhouse Bar (Venetian) has the Rock Out With Your Guac Out Challenge. A four and a half pound burrito filled with carne asada steak, pico de gallo, sautéed onions, green chiles, Cheddar cheese, fries and lettuce, wrapped in three 12-inch flour tortillas and topped with sour cream and guacamole. Eat it all in 20 minutes or less, the burrito is free plus you get $50 ROCK bucks and a t-shirt!

La Salsa Cantina (Showcase Mall & Planet Hollywood) has the El Champion Burrito Challenge. The 35 oz. burrito is a double flour tortilla filled with Mexican rice, black beans, lettuce, two fresh salsas, Jack & Cheddar cheeses, guacamole and sour cream. Finish the burrito and a 48 oz. frozen Yard Long Margarita (costs $24.95 regardless) for a free t-shirt.

RM Seafood (The Shoppes at Mandalay Bay) has Rick's Tasting Game Challenge, sixteen flavors of ice cream and sorbet that are served blind. Correctly guess them all and its free, should you fail the cost is $18.

♠♥♣♦

TIP: For Craft Brew aficionados, ask to join the Facebook Group **Las Vegas Beer & Breweries.** A great way to keep abreast of what Vegas has to offer. Discover local breweries, craft brew inspired events, deals and promotions!

TIP: Haven't tried this one yet, but check out the App Store or Google Play for the free Cityzen app. This app is a way to discover nearby locations in Vegas and other cities that offer free drinks, food and more. **www.cityzenrewards.com**

♠♥♣♦

ENTERTAINMENT VALUES

After enjoying a free or low cost meal, you may desire to sit back and relax, or perhaps follow up with some low cost entertainment. Whether your interests are to take tours, visit attractions, watch shows, check out the club scene, or participate in more active pursuits, Vegas has it all!

Similar to the previously described buffet and dining programs, there are numerous all-inclusive or discount entertainment options available. But just as with the previously described dining programs, the chapter *Saving Thousands* will provide information that will show in many cases (dependent on your situation), it can be cheaper to utilize individual coupons instead!

The following all-inclusive and discount entertainment options are available in the Las Vegas market. Although I cannot provide personal testimonials, these offers are from well-established legitimate businesses but participating venues are subject to change.

♠♥♣♦

• **Las Vegas Perks** •
http://lasvegasperks.com/
• Local 702.616.4052 •

The dining options of Las Vegas Perks were previously mentioned in the *Frugal Dining* chapter. The **Las Vegas Perks Discount Package** also includes offers for shows, tours and attractions. Las Vegas Perks is a mobile smart phone package. Offers are redeemable on Mobile Smart Phones. No App, download or printing required.

With the exception of a few offers valid for one person only, a 25% discount, or a dollar amount discount; all other offers can be used either as B1G1 or 50% off for one person. All offers are one-time use and are valid for six months from date of purchase, unless a show or venue closes. The package costs $25 and currently includes twenty-six offers for family shows, mature audience shows, tours and attractions • **Vegas the Show** • **Paranormal** • **Legends in Concert** • **V - The Ultimate Variety Show** • **Beatleshow Orchestra** • **All Shook Up Show** • **Nathan Burton Show** • **Hittsville the Show** • **50 Shades Show** • **Spoofical the Musical** • **Jeff Civillico Show** • **Popovich Comedy Pet Show** • **Chaos & Confetti** • **Mark Savard Comedy Hypnosis** • **Anthony Cools Show** • **Menopause the Musical** • **Las Vegas Live Comedy Club Show** • **Aussie Hunks Show** • **Zombie Burlesque** • **Stripper 101 Show/Class** • **Mandara Spa** • **Papillon Grand Canyon Helicopter Tour** • **Papillon Strip Helicopter Tour** • **Scenic Airlines Tour** • **CSI: The Experience** • **V Card – The Vegas Nightclub Pass** ($59 discount) •

• Las Vegas Power Pass™ •
www.lasvegaspass.com
• Toll Free 800.490.9330 •

The **Las Vegas Power Pass™** can be ordered online and delivered for an excessive $16 mailing fee, or picked up in Las Vegas at the Planet Hollywood Restaurant in Caesars Palace for FREE. Choose from:

• One day pass ($85) • Two day pass ($130) • Three day pass ($164) • Five day pass ($254) • Children's passes are also available.

The pass is valid for 12 months from date of purchase and is activated upon first use. Therefore, it is best to start using your pass first thing in the morning. The pass is valid for consecutive days only and expires at midnight on the last day. Passes are valid at each attraction once, but you can visit as many as possible in a day. At select attractions Fast Track Entry Privileges are also granted. Valid at • **High Roller** • **Eiffel Tower Experience** • **Siegfried & Roy's Secret Garden & Dolphin Habitat** • **Stratosphere Tower Observation Deck** • **The Big Apple Coaster at New York-New York** • **Voo Doo Zipline** • **Cowabunga Bay Water**

Park • Pool Party Pass • VIP Club Crawl Las Vegas • Banger Brewing Co. • Planet Hollywood Restaurant ($10 merchandise or dining credit) • TaylorMade Golf Experience • Deuce Bus Pass (24 hour) • Las Vegas Monorail (2 day pass) • Hop-On-Hop-Off Big Bus Tour (2 day pass) • Lake Mead Cruise • Hoover Dam Motor Coach Tour • Grand Canyon West Legacy Tour • Pawn Stars VIP Bus Tour • Pop Culture Walking Tour of Fremont Street• Lion Habitat Ranch • Springs Preserve • Sky Zone Trampoline Park • Las Vegas Mini Gran Prix • Gene Wood's Go Kart Racing • Kiss by Monster Mini Golf • Shalimar Wedding Chapel Experience • Countdown Las Vegas Games • Bellagio Gallery of Fine Art • Las Vegas Natural History Museum • Hollywood Cars Museum • National Atomic Testing Museum • Nevada State Museum • Erotic Heritage Museum • Museum of Fine Art • Jeff Civilico: Comedy in Action • Divas Las Vegas •

TIP: Sometimes this site runs sales. Passes can also be found on third party sites at a discount. For example, the 3-day Pass is currently available for $121.99 on **Costco.com**.

♠♥♣♦

• Go Card Las Vegas® •
www.smartdestinations.com/las-vegas-attractions-and-tours/
• Toll Free 800.887.9103 •

With the **Explorer Pass** you can visit 3 ($75), 5 ($109) or 7 ($139) attractions for one pre-paid price and save up to 55%. Alternatively, build your own pass by ordering two or more attractions at a 30% discount. You are pre-paying a discounted rate to visit each chosen attraction. Your cost and discount will depend on which attractions you choose. The passes are valid for one year from date of purchase, become activated upon first attraction visit and are valid for 30 days upon being activated. Children's passes are also available. Instant online delivery. Choose from the following • **Vegas! The Show** • **Madame Tussauds** • **Hoover Dam Tour** • **High Roller Observation Wheel Daytime Pass** • **Nathan**

Burton Comedy Magic • Stratosphere Observation Deck W/ VIP Access • Insanity, Big Shot & X-Scream at the Stratosphere • Big Bus Hop on Hop Off Day Tour • V - The Ultimate Variety Show • Planet Hollywood Restaurant (meal) • CSI: The Experience • Marvel Avengers S.T.A.T.I.O.N. • The Mob Museum • Eiffel Tower Experience • Señor Frogs (one-hour open bar) • Vegas Rockstar Club Tour • Rockstar Pool Party Tour • Las Vegas Monorail (2-Day Pass) • Zombie Burlesque • Stripper 101 (learn how to pole dance) • Beatleshow Orchestra • The Mentalist • Marc Savard Comedy Hypnosis • Chaos & Confetti Show • Popovich Comedy Pet Theater • Las Vegas Live Comedy Club • Gene Woods Racing Experience • Downtown Las Vegas Fremont Street Walking Tour •

TIP: Pass vouchers can also be found on third party sites at a discount. For example, the 3 attraction pass is currently available for $58.99 on **Living Social**.

TIP: If for any reason you do not activate your pass within a year of purchase, get a full refund! You'll have up to one year from your purchase date to return any non-activated/unused passes for a full refund.

• Pogo Pass Las Vegas Membership •
www.lasvegas.pogopass.com
• Text message 480.463.4745 •

The **Pogo Pass** costs $124.95 and there is also a $1 activation fee on the website. The membership is valid for 1 year from the date of purchase and grants free access for one person to each of the following venues • One visit to **Cowabunga Bay Water Park** • One visit to **Springs Preserve** • Two **Las Vegas 51's** baseball games • One visit to the **Discovery Children's Museum** • One visit to **BattleBlast Laser Tag** • Two visits to **Bouncy World Indoor Bounce Playland** • One visit to **Rockin' Jump** • One visit to **Nevada Climbing Centers** • One race at **Fast Lap Indoor Kart Racing** • One visit per month to **Red Rock, Santa Fe Station, Sunset**

Station and Texas Station Bowling Centers (valid for two games of bowling per location, per month) •

TIP: Pass vouchers can also be found on third party sites at a discount. For example, the pass is regularly available on **Living Social** ($49.99) and **Groupon** ($49.98).

TIP: This membership comes with a word of caution. The membership renews automatically! You must remember to cancel prior to the expiration!

♠♥♣♦

• Las Vegas Thrill Pass •
www.viator.com/tours/Las-Vegas/Viator-Exclusive-Las-Vegas-Thrill-Pass/d684-3787VTTHRILL
• Toll Free 866. 648.5873 •

Viator is a third party international travel tour and activity company. The Viator website indicates that the **Las Vegas Thrill Pass** is an exclusive offering. An Adult 2-day pre-paid pass is $94.99 and allows you to enjoy your choice of four attractions out of the following eight choices • **Voo Doo Zip Line** • **The Big Apple Coaster at New York-New York** • **Stratosphere Tower Observation Deck** & 1 ride on either **Big Shot, X-Scream** or **Insanity** • **Las Vegas Mini Gran Prix** • **Adventuredome at Circus Circus** • **Sky Zone** • **Countdown Live Escape Games** • **Gun Garage** •

CAUTION: This pass has mixed reviews. The website for the local provider (visiticket.com, also the provider of the defunct Las Vegas Meal Ticket) doesn't work and product reviews are mixed. It is highly recommended to check with your choice of venues prior to purchase and explore other coupon options detailed throughout this guide.

♠♥♣♦

Most tourists plan on taking in one or more shows when in Vegas. I can still remember my days as a casino employee, walking the casino floor on concert evenings in the hours leading up to an event, randomly passing out unsold concert tickets! No one likes to see empty seats. Not the performers, the management, or the audience! A filled seat improves the ambiance of an event and in turn the overall experience! Who knows, one day you might be the recipient of one of those complimentary unsold tickets, but until that time there are numerous show ticket discount options available.

A good source for FREE coupons that offer show discounts are the FREE tourist magazines that are provided in your hotel room, or available in racks by the bell desk in hotel lobbies. These include *Las Vegas Magazine*, *The Sunday*, *Vegas2Go*™, *Showbiz Weekly*, *Where Quick Guides*, *Las Vegas Spotlight* and *24/7 Magazine* among others.

Although the variety of shows available can be inconsistent, you can find discounted show tickets on **Living Social**, **Groupon**, **Travel Zoo**, **Viator** and **The Radio Shopping Show**sm . The coupon sources to be discussed in the *Saving Thousands* chapter also offer a wide variety of free, B1G1 and 50% off show tickets.

♠♥♣♦

• **Tickets for Tonight** •
www.tix4tonight.com
• Toll Free 877.849.4868 •

Tix4Tonight is probably the number one source for discount same day show tickets in Las Vegas. The company carries tickets to over 100 Vegas shows and attractions every day, at big discounts. But because they sell unsold seats for the day's shows, inventory varies daily (posted online in the morning) and popular shows can sell out quickly. By the time booths open at 10 AM every morning, people have already been queuing up!

Discount tickets (for that specific days shows only) are sold out of booth locations on the Strip and Downtown • **Grand Bazaar Shops @ Bally's** • **Planet Hollywood** • **Showcase Mall** • **Giant Coke Bottle @ Showcase Mall** • **Casino Royale** • **Fashion Show Mall** • **Circus Circus** • **Slots of Fun** • **Four Queens** • **Town Square Mall** •

♠♥♣♦

• Goldstar •
www.goldstar.com/las-vegas/

Goldstar is another source of tickets for theater, concerts, comedy, sports and attractions in Las Vegas. Goldstar advertises half-price and members-only complimentary tickets to the best events in Vegas. Membership is free with valid email address sign-up. Purchased tickets are either delivered digitally or available for pick-up at "Will Call."

Browsing the Goldstar website it is apparent that they provide discount ticket options for numerous venues including The Smith Center for the Performing Arts, Thomas & Mack Center and Orleans Arena. There is also a variety of casino shows and attractions in inventory, including • **Penn & Teller** • **Donny & Marie Osmond** • **Wet 'n' Wild** • **High Roller at The LINQ** •

• Fill a Seat •
www.fillaseatlasvegas.com
• Local 702.690.9327 •

FILLASEAT™ is the members-only seat filling service. When theaters, concerts, sporting events and festivals need to fill the seats of unsold tickets, they are offered for free to FILLASEAT™ **local members** (tickets are given to locals because they are not considered the primary market). For a Las Vegas membership you must be at least 21 and a local resident with a valid Nevada ID, or a Military ID and stationed in Southern Nevada. Memberships are valid for 1-year from the date of purchase. Limited to one show per day. Only members can see a list of available shows. All memberships are non-refundable.

The Duet Membership (1↔2 tickets per event) is $89.95, a Quartet Membership (1↔4 tickets) costs $159.95, either is $20 off for seniors 60 and over.

TIP: The website sometimes runs membership promotions. Recently the "7 Year Anniversary Special" offered all memberships for $55.55! Also check **Living Social** or **Groupon** as memberships are frequently sold at half-off!

♠♥♣♦

In addition to the countless show options available in Vegas, the nightlife scene extends to bar and nightclub venues, which are extremely vibrant and competitive. More than thirty casino properties offer one or more bar and nightclub venues for those so inclined! The frugal traveler or resident can also benefit from discounts, coupons and pass options at nightlife venues!

• V Card •
www.vcardlasvegas.com
• Toll Free 866.932.1818 •

The **Vegas Nightlife Pass** or **V Card**, provides complimentary admission through the VIP line at Las Vegas nightclubs, lounges, gentlemen's clubs, day clubs and pools. The V Card costs $149.99, $162.21 including taxes and fees. You can purchase the V Card either online or by visiting the V Theater Box Office in person at Planet Hollywood Resort & Casino" Miracle Mile Shops. When ordering online, you can pick it up from the box office when you arrive in Vegas.

The card can be used once at each venue (with provided entry cards), and does not have an expiration date, but will expire when all your "entry cards" are exhausted. Pass is valid at • **Tao Nightclub** • **Marquee Nightclub** (Mondays) • **Hyde Nightclub** • **LAX Nightclub** • **Chateau Nightclub** • **Ghostbar** • **VooDoo Lounge** • **The Ainsworth** • **PBR Rockbar** • **Rockhouse** • **McFadden's** • **Rehab** • **Tao Beach** • **Hard Rock Beach Life** • **Palms Place Pool** • **Palms Pool & Bungalows** • **Marquee Day Club** (Fridays) • **Azure** • **GBDC** (Saturday) • **Venus European Pool Club** • **Sapphire Day Club & Pool** •**Hustler Topless Bar** • **Sapphire** • **Treasures** (2 for 1 dining) • **OG** • **Cheetahs** • **Spearmint Rhino** • **Crazy Horse III** •**Topless Déjà vu Showgirls** • **Sake Rok at the Park** • **Vanguard Lounge** (unlimited use) •

TIP: The Vegas Nightlife Pass is typically available from **Goldstar**, **Living Social**, **Groupon** and **Destination Coupons** at a third the cost!

♠♥♣♦

♠♥♣♦

● Vegas Party Band ●
www.nightclubs.com
www.vegaspartyband.com
● No phone contact information ●

The **Vegas Party Band** is a wristband valid for access to over 20 nightclubs, pool parties and strip clubs for a one week period. The cost for the wristband is $79.95 and it is valid at ● **Embassy Nightclub** ● **VooDoo Lounge** ● **Ghostbar** ● **Hyde** ● **LAX** ● **Chateau** ● **Foxtail Nightclub** ● **FIZZ** ● **Foundation Room** ● **Artisan Nightclub** ● **Palms Pool** ● **Rehab** ● **Sky Beach Club** ● **Sapphire Pool** ● **Crazy Horse III** ● **Larry Flynt's Hustler Club** ● **Sapphire Treasures** ●

TIP: On vegaspartyband.com try the code NC55 for $20 off! Or, on occasion a pop-up screen will appear on the site for a $30 off code via email.

TIP: Presidential Limousine of Las Vegas, the official limo for Vegas Party Band and Nightclubs.com, offers an "additional 10% off the lowest limo rates." **www.presidentiallimolv.com**

SAVING THOUSANDS

♠♥♣♦

I am reminded of the story of a visitor to Las Vegas from an impoverished third world country. Having heard his entire life how lavish, extravagant, affluent and decadent Americans were, a visual image had been developed of how easily money could be had on the streets of America. After many years of scrimping and saving, the man finally saved enough to travel to the United States where he would hopefully share in the great wealth the country had to offer.

Arriving at McCarran International Airport exhausted, the man exited the terminal in order to take a city bus to his motel. On his way to the bus stop the man noticed a twenty dollar bill laying in the street and thought . . . I am so very, very tired from my travels . . . I will start picking up the money in the street tomorrow.

The moral of the story is don't put it off until tomorrow, start picking up the free money available in the streets of Las Vegas today! To be honest, similar to our friend in the preceding story, I have found a great deal of money in the streets and on the floor of casinos in Vegas, in increments ranging from a penny to $600! The difference being, that I've stopped and picked it up! However, the "free money" referenced in this chapter comes not in the form of cash, but in the form of coupons, rewards and discounts.

♠♥♣♦

Without realizing it, you may already be on the path to saving money in Las Vegas! If you're a member of a hotel loyalty program or credit card holder from **Hilton HHonors**, **Starwood Preferred Guest**, **Marriott Rewards** or some other hotelier, rewards can be used and earned while in Vegas! Also, don't overlook any memberships you have that provide discounts at Las Vegas venues. AARP and AAA are good examples, both have participating venue information and discounts posted online.

♠♥♣♦

In "old" Vegas, almost every casino offered a coupon "fun book" to entice customers into their casino. Today very few "fun book" promotions exist, of those that do, most are offered to hotel guests upon check-in. Some hotels still provide a form of coupons upon registration (ranging from one or two, a sheet, or a booklet of coupons).

This is not to say coupons are no longer available in the Vegas market. To the contrary, the use of coupons is as prevalent as before, if not more so. A few good sources for free coupons are free tourist magazines and flyers that are provided in your hotel room, or available in racks by the bell desk in hotel lobbies. These include *Las Vegas Magazine*, *The Sunday*, *Vegas2Go*™, *Showbiz Weekly*, *Where Quick Guides*, *Las Vegas Spotlight* and *24/7 Magazine* among others. Coupons found in these free tourist magazines are typically from the same advertisers. In these magazines you can expect to find basic coupons for small discounts and promotions on dining, shows, attractions, shops and the Monorail.

Coupons are also distributed on the Strip and pedestrian walkways. On occasion, Caesars Entertainment hands out coupons for the **Mac King Comedy Show** and **Carnival World Buffet** among others, at the Carnival Court located between Harrah's and The LINQ, or ask at the Harrah's Players Club desk. For locals, Caesars Entertainment posts coupons for discounts on shows, meals, spa treatments, attractions and gift shops online at:
www.caesars.com/las-vegas/deals/locals

CAUTION: Booths with hawkers on Las Vegas Boulevard, Fremont Street Experience and inside many businesses, will be offering free show, buffet or attraction tickets, even free future vacations. These are time-share promotions which require, should you survive the initial screening process, your attendance at a high pressure sales presentation that lasts a few hours. Money managers advise that buying into a time-share unit is typically a bad financial decision. Taking into consideration the value of your limited time in Vegas, these "freebies" may not be worth the effort and risk. This guide covers much safer and easier freebie options!

♠♥♣♦

If you plan on shopping in Vegas, every mall and outlet offers a coupon booklet featuring dining and retail establishments at their venue. Most are readily provided just by asking, some may require an easily attainable coupon, or that you are a non-resident.

• Fashion Show Mall •
Premier Passport is available from the Concierge Center on the lower lever outside Macy's.

• Grand Canal Shops at The Venetian & Palazzo•
Premier Passport is available from the Apothecary, Brighton or Welcome to Las Vegas Stores.

• Miracle Mile Shops at Planet Hollywood •
Shop Dine Save Coupon Book is available from Customer Service.

• The Forum Shops at Caesars Palace •
VIP Special Offer Booklet is available from Concierge Service Centers near the Fountain of the Gods and on the second level by the spiral escalator.

• Town Square •
Town Square Rewards is available from the Town Square Concierge, on the Town Square free shuttle and at many hotel concierge desks. If you plan on shopping a lot, Town Square also has a customer loyalty program called Inner Square Rewards! Earn rewards for shopping!

• Las Vegas Premium Outlets • North & South •
Savings Passport is available from Simon Guest Services or the Information Center. Coupon for *Savings Passport* is found in free tourist magazines.

• Fashion Outlets at Primm, Nevada •
Green Savings Card is available at Fashion Outlets Customer Service Center located in the food court with ad found in free tourist magazines. Located on I-15 south of Las Vegas.

♠♥♣♦

It is worth reiterating that for those not accustomed to using coupons or discount options, don't be shy or embarrassed about taking advantage of the plethora of opportunities available! There is no stigma attached to the use of coupons or seeking discounts. In fact, it is normal and expected behavior. Coupons, promotions and discounts are marketing tools utilized by most Las Vegas casinos, hotels, restaurants and show venues!

TIP: When planning your use of coupons, remember that most coupons are NOT VALID on Holidays or weekends (typically Friday & Saturday).

♠♥♣♦

Free Online Coupons
There are many sites online that provide free coupons for Vegas businesses, just download and/or print them out!

• ValPak •
www.valpak.com/coupons/savings/all/las+vegas/nv

Better known for the Blue Envelope of coupons mailed to millions of targeted households in 45 states and 4 Canadian provinces, **Valpak's** digital advertising program provides targeted neighborhood business offers and opportunities.

Browse through local restaurant offers, home and office retailers, personal care and automotive deals. Virtual coupon boxes provide the local company name, the offer, an option to print, a rollover box with the exact address of the coupon location and other locations the coupon may be valid at.

A recent search showed 130 Las Vegas offers including • **Denny's** • **Las Vegas Philharmonic** • **Big Ern's BBQ** (in Container Park Downtown) • **Papillon Grand Canyon Helicopters** • **Jersey Mike's Subs** • **Earl of Sandwich** • **Capriotti's Sandwich Shop** • **Wolfgang Puck Bar & Grill** • **Mt. Charleston Resort** •

TIP: Also available as a free app through Google Play.

• Vegas 4 Locals •
www.vegas4locals.com/coupons

Contrary to what the name implies, this site is loaded with free coupons for everyone! Offers include discounted show tickets, special deals on tours & attractions, auctions, community resources. Save on show tickets, tours, local attractions, dining, nightlife, health & wellness, shopping and more. A small sampling of recent offerings includes:
• Carlos' n Charlie's • Casa di Amore • Hennessey's Tavern • Pampas Brazilian Grille • Pawn Stars VIP Tour • Papillon Helicopter Tours • CSI: The Experience • Donny & Marie • Nathan Burton Comedy Magic • Aussie Heat •

Just print the coupons that you want, or in many cases show the offer on your mobile device to the merchant or venue.

• Destination Coupons •
www.destinationcoupons.com/nevada/las_vegas/las-vegas-coupons.asp

Destination Coupons provides free travel discounts, mobile-friendly coupons and promo codes for over 7,000 destinations worldwide. In the Vegas market, Destination Coupons has the widest selection of ticket discounts, half-price tickets, coupons, promo codes and discount codes! Venues include shows, hotels, restaurants & buffets, tours, transportation, golfing, gaming, nightlife and shopping. Not a third party vendor, you buy direct from official show websites and venues.

A small sampling of recent offerings includes • **Las Vegas Monorail** • **Super Shuttle** • **Nine Car Rental Agencies** • **Uber** • **Papillon Helicopter Tours** • **Big Bus Hop-On Hop-Off Tours** • **Gun Garage** • **High Roller at the LINQ** • **Madame Tussauds** ••**The Mob Museum** • **Las Vegas Mini Gran Prix** • **Planet Hollywood Restaurant** at Caesars Palace • **Carlos' n Charlie's** • **Spice Market Buffet** • **Tournament of Kings** at Excalibur • **Beatleshow Orchestra** • **Carrot Top** • **Chippendales** • **Fantasy at Luxor** •

♠♥♣♦

Social Media

Many casinos have jumped on the social media bandwagon by offering free online games. Anyone 18 or older can play these games for free. Players also have the option of purchasing chips to play with, but it is not required as they all offer free chips daily. These casino social media sites link your free social media account to your Players Club account, rewarding you with comps and discounts at their properties! However, the first two options reward nothing to very little unless you actually purchase chips.

• Playtika Games •
https://www.caesars.com/play

The first to introduce free-to-play casino-style games to social networks was Caesars Entertainment's online games unit Playtika, which offers: • **Slotomania** • **House of Fun** • **Caesars Slots** • **Vegas Downtown Slots** • **Bingo Blitz** • **World Series of Poker** •

By playing these games on Facebook, you can earn CET Total Rewards Credits. However, changes may be in store for the social program. In July 2016 CET agreed to a sale of the Playtika unit for $4.4 billion to Chinese investors! The sale did not include the World Series of Poker brand or the online WSOP real-money gambling platform.

♠♥♣♦

• STN Play •
https://play.sclv.com

Red Rock Resorts, under the Station Casinos brand, had previously been a reward partner on Playstudios Games' social media casino game platform, but ended that relationship at the beginning of this year. Station Casinos is the latest to join the casino games social media bandwagon with the recent launch of their social media game site **STN Play**. The site offers a wide selection of games including slots and video poker.

♠♥♣♦

• Playstudios Games •
www.playstudios.com

Hands down, Playstudios Games offers the best free casino social games. Playstudios is also the best source for Vegas coupons, actually "rewards," that can be acquired for free playing online social media games and mobile apps!

If you have limited time to play online, the best social media casino game sites and rewards are offered by **Playstudios** in association with • **MGM Resorts International** (eleven Las Vegas properties) • **Resorts World International** • **Couples Resorts** • **Departure Lounge** • **Royal Caribbean International** • **MSC Cruises** • **Cirque du Soleil** • **The Smith Center** • **T-Mobile Arena** • **The Mob Museum** • **Madame Tussauds** • **Casa de Shenandoah** • **Maverick Helicopters** • **Gray Line Tours** • **Segway Las Vegas Tours** • **Pole Position** • **House of Blues** • **Wolfgang Puck** (eight locations) • **Hexx** • **Beer Park** • **Las Vegas Monorail** •

Nothing in life is totally free (you'll have to invest time to accumulate free play chips), but you do have the option to play Playstudios games for FREE, or you can purchase chips to play with. Either way, the rewards for playing these games range from FREE rooms with the payment of the daily resort fee; B1G1 appetizers, desserts, buffets and entrees; up to and including free buffets, drinks, helicopter tours and much more! Reward offerings are constantly being refreshed and augmented!

Either purchase or obtain free purple chips (VP) which are used to play the various games in order to earn gold Loyalty Points (LP). Free chips are accumulated through daily free spins, bonus codes, coupon codes and sign-ins (every 4 hours you can acquire free chips, every 2 hours on **Pop! Slots**)! Purple chip balances are game specific, and have no value except to allow you to play the games. The purpose of playing these games is to acquire gold Loyalty Points which are used to purchase rewards!

The basic game to start out with is the Facebook version of **myVEGAS™ Slots**. Once you've set up the Facebook game, the mobile game apps can be linked with the Facebook version and your Loyalty Point balances will be synchronized. Once synchronized, your LP balance will increase more rapidly because it will represent the total LP from all five games:

- myVEGAS™ Slots Facebook Game •
- myVEGAS™ Slots Mobile App •
- myVEGAS™ Blackjack Mobile App •
- myKONAMI Slots™ Mobile App & Facebook Game •
- myVEGAS™ POP! Slots Mobile App •

In July 2016 Playstudios released **POP! Slots,** their fifth free casino game in the form of a mobile application. Similar to Playstudios' original games, **POP! Slots** offers in-app purchases but can be played totally free with bi-hourly and daily free chip bonuses.

TIP: Free chip and coupon codes are obtained by "liking" the myVEGAS page on Facebook. Some free chip and coupon codes expire after a certain number of players redeem the codes, but most expire after a few weeks.

TIP: A great third party source for codes that may still be valid is the Facebook page of **James Hite**. Just click on the links provided for free play chips in the Facebook game! Free play chip codes are also provided for the three mobile games! To acquire many free play chips when you first start to play these games, on James Hite's page scroll down to "Previous Mobile Codes" and "Previous Coupons." Simply enter the codes in the appropriate mobile game and click on the coupon links until you reach outdated or invalid coupons or codes. You will amass a great deal of free play chips! Don't forget to follow James Hite on Facebook for daily code updates!

It would take volumes to describe the ins and outs of playing these games (a project for another day), but basic play should become self- evident. There are also small help sections available within each game. Sometimes answers to possible questions will also appear on the **myVEGAS Facebook Page**.

The rewards available for purchase with your earned Loyalty Points include Free or discount room nights at MGM Properties, Free or B1G1 buffets and dining options at MGM Resorts, B1G1 Monorail Tickets, Free helicopter tours, Free drinks, Free Show tickets, Free cruises and much more!

♠♥♣♦

• Cannery Casinos webPASS Games •
www.eastsidecannery.com/webpass
www.canerycasino.com/webpass

The **Eastside Cannery webPASS** and **Cannery webPASS** programs are free online promotional sites where you can acquire coupons for free or discount goods and services at each casino property. Free to join, a CAN Club Players Club account is not required to join or play, but in order to redeem rewards, your online webPASS account must be connected to your CAN Club account. Each property has its own separate CAN Club and webPASS program. Earnings and rewards are not interchangeable between properties.

Earn webCREDITS (virtual currency) by completing activities online or on your mobile device. Activities include daily login; inviting a friend; featured promotions; single question surveys; trivia questions; arcade and casino game play (played for fun not money). Credits are quick and easy to accumulate in a short period. Once you've signed-up you typically receive the Bonus Code "WELCOME," which when entered is good for 2,500 webCREDITS! Try the code "WEBPASS" as well, might still be worth 25,000!

Spend earned webCREDITS on rewards that include free casino Slot play with minimal play; Table Game match play; cocktails; hotel room upgrade or add-ons; free or B1G1 buffets; dining discounts or free menu items and more! Upper level rewards include breakfast in bed; lunch with the General Manager and for a million credits, choose the color of the building or put a message on the marquee!

To claim rewards you need to print vouchers, which will expire in 7 days. Before the voucher expires, it needs to be exchanged at the corresponding properties CAN Club

Center for your reward coupon. You are limited to one of each voucher type per month. Only one voucher, regardless of type, can be redeemed per day.

CAUTION: Both Cannery properties were purchased by Boyd Gaming during 2016. The transition and rebranding of the properties into the Boyd group is under way. Whether the webPASS program will be continued or phased out is uncertain. Enjoy the benefits while you can!

♠♥♣♦

• Las Vegas Advisor Casino •
https://play.lasvegasadvisor.com/

The **Las Vegas Advisor Casino** is an online site where you can play Blackjack, Poker and other casino games for free. The site is a product of the Las Vegas Advisor (to be discussed shortly). You do not need to be a Las Vegas Advisor Member to sign-up and play. Sign-up is free and you get $250,000 in free play chips.

One Sunday per month a free Texas Hold'em *Sunday Funday Poker Tournament* is held at noon Pacific Time, 3 PM Eastern Time. You play live against other real players. First place typically wins $100 cash and the top fourteen places also get prizes, including Las Vegas Advisor membership, books, merchandise and gift cards.

♠♥♣♦

Paying for Coupons

Another great source for Las Vegas coupons is to purchase them! The two best sources for purchased Vegas coupons are a Las Vegas Advisor Membership which includes a coupon book, and the travel guide *The American Casino Guide*.

• Huntington Press •
www.lasvegasadvisor.com
• Local 702.252.0655 • 800.244.2224 •

The **Las Vegas Advisor Membership** is a __recommended must have__ for both tourists and locals! Membership benefits include some of the best Vegas coupons, deals and discounts available! You do not need to be a member to access the free Las Vegas Advisor website, which is an excellent source for current information about Las Vegas deals, discounts, promotions and travel information.

Membership provides an exclusive monthly newsletter (one per month for one year, MAILED via first-class postage); the *Member Rewards Book (MRB)* coupon booklet; an ongoing program of downloadable deals at CouponsInVegas.com; and access to other exclusive premium content and forums at LasVegasAdvisor.com. Yearly membership is $50 plus $3.50 for domestic shipping and handling.

TIP: An online membership is also available for just $37 plus $3.50 for domestic shipping of the *MRB*! The only difference is that you do not receive a hard copy of the newsletter, but you can access it online for free!

TIP: You can save the shipping cost by picking up your *MRB* during business hours at the Huntington Press office located at 3665 Procyon Street, roughly one block north of the RIO!

There is a limit of one membership/*MRB* per person, per year; two per household (must be in individual names). Coupons expire on various dates between December 23 and December 31, 2017. Most coupons (except gaming) are valid for two people (B1G1). Therefore, with two memberships a couple can visit each venue twice! However, in order to utilize the high value gaming coupons, you will each need a membership (highly recommended).

To use a coupon you will be required to have a Players Club account at the casino where the coupon will be honored. Casinos limit the use of *MRB* coupons to one per person/per year and track whether you have previously used the offer by linking it's redemption to your Players Club account.

The *MRB* typically includes a few coupons that can be used for lodging discounts and around thirty buffet coupons. If you get tired of buffets, the *MRB* also typically includes over thirty café and restaurant dining coupons as well as free drink coupons! If you're feeling adventurous or want to take in some attractions, the *MRB* provides some options.

No visit to Vegas is complete without taking in a show or two, the *MRB* typically contains nearly twenty show coupons (mainly B1G1 or 50% off)! Of these, some offer Free Tickets with a minimum drink purchase or box office charge! Venues include • **V Theater** • **Saxe Theater** • **Luxor** • **Harrah's** • **Golden Nugget** • **Binion's** • **Tropicana** •

By using just a few of the coupons in the *MRB*, you will recoup the cost of membership! But the real monetary value of a Las Vegas Advisor Membership is contained within the gaming coupons. By using a fraction of these coupons (and walking away once you've completed the offer) you can easily recoup double or triple the cost of membership! The *MRB* gaming coupons include free or match Slot play, table game match play and various other bonus offers.

TIP: If you are going to purchase coupons from only one source, this is it! If you are not planning on going to Vegas until December, wait until then to purchase a membership. At the end of the year you can typically get a trial Las Vegas Advisor Membership w/*MRB* for just $15! Remember, *MRB* coupons will expire at the end of the year and do not remove coupons from the booklet prior to redemption!

TIP: You do <u>not</u> have to be a Las Vegas Advisor Member in order to visit and peruse the Las Vegas Advisor website. Certain areas are reserved for members only, but there is a great deal of information available online. A few words of caution; the website has recently been rebuilt and contains some advertising pop-ups which can be irritating; and a great deal of the information appears outdated, which is the same problem all Vegas websites seem to experience!

♠♥♣♦

• 2017 American Casino Guide •
www.americancasinoguide.com

Another great source for Las Vegas coupons is the *American Casino Guide*, which can be purchased online directly from the publisher with a 100% money back guarantee. Also available through Amazon, bookstores and at Gambler's General Store on 800 South Main Street in Downtown Vegas.

Some coupons are duplicates of those offered through the Las Vegas Advisor *MRB*, but there are numerous other offers exclusive to the *American Casino Guide*. If you have two similar coupons, one from the *MRB* and another from the *American Casino Guide,* you can use them both!

The *American Casino Guide* is <u>the</u> source for new member Players Club sign-up promotional coupons. If the casino is also running a sign-up promotion, typically you can take advantage of both offers! Coupons for new Players Club members include • **Aliante** • **Longhorn** • **California**, **Fremont & Main Street Station** (play $25 on Slots or Video Poker and get $10 in Free Play) • **Golden Gate** • **Sam's Town** • **SLS** •

Gaming coupons valid for all Players Club members include offers from: •**Aliante** • **Binion's** • **The D** • **Downtown Grand** • **Ellis Island** • **Four Queens** • **Gold Coast** • **Golden Gate** • **Hooters** • **Longhorn** • **Orleans** • **The Palms** • **Plaza** • **Rampart** • **Suncoast** • **Tuscany** •

An expanding trend in the *American Casino Guide* are gaming coupons where you earn a minimal amount of points playing Slots or Video Poker and receive a free breakfast, lunch or dinner buffet and keep the points! There are 10 coupons from • **California** • **Fremont** • **Main Street Station** • **Sam's Town** • **Gold Coast** • **South Point** •

The *American Casino Guide* also contains B1G1 buffet coupons for • **Aliante** • **Arizona Charlie's Boulder & Decatur** • **Boulder Station** • **Fiesta Henderson & Rancho** • **Golden Nugget** • **Palace Station** • **Rampart** • **Santa Fe Station** • **Silver Sevens** • **Silverton** • **Suncoast** • **Green Valley Ranch Resort** • **Red Rock Resort** • **Sunset Station** • **Texas Station** • Two additional buffet coupons offer $5 off per person at the **Carnival World Buffet at the Rio** and $10 off per person for the **Carnival World Buffet Seafood Buffet** (both offers are good for up to 4 people).

The *American Casino Guide* is a great source for casino café coupons: • 2-for-1 hamburger at **Binion's Café** • $10 worth of food for $5 at the **Grand Café** at **Boulder Station & Texas**

Station • $10 dining credit towards purchase of $20 or more at the **Grand Café** in **Red Rock Resort, Green Valley Ranch, Fiesta Henderson** & **Fiesta Rancho•**

No Vegas coupon book would be complete without show discounts and the *American Casino Guide* doesn't disappoint. B1G1 coupons are included for tickets to • **Mike Hammer** • **Defending the Caveman** • **Laughternoon** • **X Comedy** • **Legends in Concert** • **Gordie Brown Live!** • **Spirit of the King Elvis Tribute Show** • **Mac King (2 free with drink purchase)** • **X Rocks** •

In addition, B1G1 coupons are included for showroom tickets at **The Orleans** and for any show at **V-Theater** or **Saxe Theater** located in the Miracle Mile Shops at Planet Hollywood!

There are numerous other dining, drink, attraction and room coupons available in the *American Casino Guide*, for Las Vegas, Laughlin and beyond! For a complete listing visit **www.americancasinoguide.com/2017-american-casino-guide-coupon-list.html**

TIP: The American Casino Guide website hosts a weekly post from Scot Krause, whom supplies updated information each Sunday on Las Vegas casino promotions. **http://www.americancasinoguide.com/vegas-values.html**

FRUGAL GAMING

Almost every tourist visits Las Vegas to experience the famous Las Vegas Boulevard by taking in the sights, enjoying its attractions, watching world class shows and experiencing countless fine dining options. But the frugal gambler comprehends that his gaming dollar is better spent elsewhere! Mathematically, you should attain a better return on your gaming dollar by playing at off-Strip casinos.

Billions of dollars are invested to build and operate casinos. These ventures do not depend on luck to generate income and profits. In fact, casinos make money on their games because of the mathematics behind the games. A casino is guaranteed to win in the long run, by having a built in advantage (house edge) on every bet placed! With but few exceptions, over time the house always wins because of the mathematical advantage it enjoys over the player.

Because gaming is a regulated business, the Nevada Gaming Commission and the Nevada Gaming Control Board govern the gaming industry through strict regulation of all persons, locations, practices and related activities. Through their official website, information on gaming statutes, regulations and statistics is provided the public. **www.gaming.nv.gov**

The *Monthly & Annual Gaming Revenue Reports* posted on this website provide statewide, countywide, and area data on the "win percent" for each game of chance played in Nevada casinos. The "win percent" for Slot devices (Slots, Video Poker and Video Keno) is a ratio which represents the reported win amount divided by the total dollar amount played by patrons. The August 2016 report indicates that for all non-restricted gaming locations statewide, the win percentage was 12.07% for Table Games and 6.92% for Slots. This means that for every $1.00 of coin-in on Slots in August, casinos paid-out just a fraction over 93¢!

By looking at the reported total "win percentage" by area, it is easy to determine where you can theoretically get more play for your gaming dollar. Of the three main Las Vegas reporting areas (Las Vegas Strip, Downtown and Boulder Strip), in August 2016 the Las Vegas Strip had the highest "win percentages" (11.71% Table Games / 7.95% Slots), Downtown had the lowest win percentage for Table Games (11.38%) and Boulder Strip the lowest win percentage for Slots (6.94%). Although the actual percentages change monthly, typically the areas with the lowest and highest win percentages don't.

The above total win percentages are an average of all games. Every game type, whether a Table Game or Slot device, has its own win percentage. For example, Megabucks has the highest Slot win percentage. In July 2016 the percentage was 13.65%, within its typical range. During a month when a Megabucks jackpot(s) is hit, the percentage will of course drop drastically.

Slot win percentages are reported by a games denomination. In comparison to Megabucks, in July other $1 denomination Slots on the Las Vegas Strip averaged 7.18%. It may be surprising to some, but the next highest win percentage for casinos was on the 1¢ denomination, 11.18% on the Las Vegas Strip! The lowest Slot win percentage on the Las Vegas Strip was on $5 denomination devices, at 5.46%.

The difference in some win percentages may appear minor, but to put these numbers into perspective, the *Abbreviated Revenue Release* indicates that Nevada's non-restricted gaming licensees reported a total "gaming win" of $860,696,184 just for the month of August 2016!

Of all the games of chance offered in Las Vegas the lowest win percentage for casinos is Bingo (-3.46% Statewide / -4.02% Las Vegas Strip / -9.23 % Boulder Strip - 8/2016). This means that for every $1.00 wagered on Bingo in August 2016, casinos on the Boulder Strip paid-out just a fraction over $1.09!

As can be seen by the numbers, casinos use Bingo as a loss leader, the marketing principle used by grocery and retail stores selling a product at or below cost to attract customers. The expectation is that the Bingo player will expend other money on food, beverage and gaming in their casino, before and after the Bingo session. It is also typical that a players spouse will play Slots or Video Poker instead of Bingo, while waiting for their partner's session to end.

After Bingo, the games with the lowest win percentage for casinos are 21 (Blackjack), Baccarat and Mini Baccarat, all with roughly the same house edge. The highest win percentages for the casino, therefore the worst for the consumer, are 3-Card Poker, Keno, Let it Ride and Craps.

♠♥♣♦

In simple terms, what this means to you is that in order to get more play from your gambling dollar, choose where you play and what you play wisely. If you're going to gamble, the best advice is to learn basic game strategy first; pick a Slot denomination or table wager amount that you are comfortable with; set a budget for gambling, and stay within that limit. Look upon gambling as an entertainment expense, if you win in the long run even better! If you lose, the cost for that entertainment is limited to the amount you budgeted.

How much time you plan on gambling and how much you budget for that entertainment depends on your personal situation. The Convention and Visitors Authority reported that in 2015 73% of Las Vegas visitors gambled an average of 2.9 hours per day. Of those visitors who gambled, the average gambling budget was $578. You can budget more or less dependent on your circumstances, but the *Saving Thousands* chapter will show how to enjoy yourself gambling and budget much, much less!

Regardless of the amount of your gambling budget, before you put your bankroll at risk by placing your first Table Game or Slot device wager, sign-up for the casinos loyalty program, known as a Players Club.

♠♥♣♦

PLAYERS CLUBS

Similar to travel and retail loyalty programs, almost every casino offers a Players Club program to its customers. In the case of multiple casinos being owned and operated by single corporations, you only need to join their Players Club once, in order to earn and enjoy privileges at all their connected properties. MGM Resorts International's Players Club program is **Mlife**, Caesars Entertainment has **Total Rewards**, Boyd Gaming uses **B Connected** and Red Rock Resorts (Station Casinos) has the **Boarding Pass**. There are over forty Players Clubs in the Las Vegas valley!

Free to join, most clubs offer a sign-up promotion or bonus. Promotional sign-up bonuses can range from a free gift, free points, free Slot play, or even the return of your first days gambling losses (in free Slot play)! Some clubs also offer coupons with additional sign-up bonuses, which can be combined with an ongoing promotion (see *Savings Thousands* chapter)!

As a club member you earn program comps (a complimentary) based on the amount you spend in the casino, irrespective of how much you win or lose. Comps come in the form of free Slot play, food, drinks, rooms, show tickets, gifts and even cash. Most casinos also provide for discretionary comps through management, a Supervisor, Pit Boss or Casino Host. Typically, discretionary comps are reserved for larger or more frequent players and will not be discussed here.

♠♥♣♦

If you have already signed-up at your local area casino for an MGM, Caesars, Boyd Gaming or Penn National Gaming Players Club in another state, you are already on the path to receiving Las Vegas complimentaries! Any points you have already earned on your club card in another location are also valid for redemption in Las Vegas!

Another method to quickly accumulate Players Club points, rewards and complimentaries for your Las Vegas travel, is to apply for, and use, a casino sanctioned credit card.

Caesars Entertainment offers the **Total Rewards Visa**. Use of the card will earn points credited to your Players Club account. Sign-up bonuses: your choice of two buffet passes, two high roller tickets, two show tickets or one night stay; plus Total Rewards Players Club upgrade to Platinum Status with first purchase; and earn 10,000 bonus points after spending $750 at non-Total Rewards venues in the first 90 days! **https://www.totalrewards.com/content/cet-tr/en/earn-and-redeem/with-tr-alliances/tr-visa.html?rd=CL1_visa**

MGM Resorts International offers the **Mlife Rewards Mastercard**. Use of the card will earn points credited to your Players Club account. Sign-up bonuses: automatic Mlife Players Club upgrade to Pearl Status (benefits include free self-parking, buffet line pass and priority check-in at all Mlife resorts; and earn 10,000 bonus points after spending $1,000 in the first 3 billing cycles. **https://www.mlife.com/en/overview/mlife-rewards-mastercard.html**

♠♥♣♦

Casinos have an earning potential on each Players Club member, referred to as player value or theoretical win. In the Slot department, this value is easily tracked and determined by your actual play, known as coin-in.

At most casinos, for every dollar of coin-in on a Slot device, you accumulate one point in your Players Club account. On Video Poker machines, it takes one, two or more dollars (dependent on the game variation and casino) of coin-in to earn one point.

Some casinos offer multiple point promotions (2X, 3X, 7X, 15X points) on certain days of the week and on holidays. Point multiplier promotions are worth looking for and taking advantage of, as comp dollars can add up fast! Earned points can then be turned into comps at various rates of exchange dependent on casino.

♠♥♣♦

In Table Games, your player value is calculated by a mathematical formula. Using the house advantage of a game, average bet size, duration of play and pace of the game (decisions per hour), a casino can determine how much it expects to win from a certain player. Many casinos set comp (complimentary) policies by giving the player back a set percentage of their earning potential. Comp and rebate policies based on theoretical loss are the most popular, but rebates on actual losses are still used by some casinos.

Player tracking data is required by the casino in order to reward you with all the comps your play deserves. To accomplish this, Players Clubs utilize a plastic Players Card (similar to a debit card) that can record every dollar spent in the casino, whether in retail outlets, on amenities, food & beverage, lodging or gaming. But, only the purchases and play recorded on the card earn complimentaries! Therefore, every dollar you spend or gamble should be recorded! Always insert a Players Card in a Slot or Video Poker machine and present it at Table Games, hotel registration, restaurants, bars and even shops!

♠♥♣♦

Your Players Club data will also be utilized by the casino's marketing department. You will periodically receive offers and advertisements just for signing-up. Dependent on your play, you will receive offers for future visits and events. These offers are tailored to locals and tourists. If you are an out-of-state visitor for example, you can expect to receive free, B1G1 or waived resort fee hotel room offers that may even include free play or food credits.

TIP: To increase the value of future offers, concentrate play during your trip at just a few casinos. Your gaming budget played at a few casinos will receive better offers than the same amount wagered at many casinos! Sign-up at every casino where you gamble during your visit, have a coupon, or that offers a good promotion.

TIP: Another reason for not signing-up willy-nilly for every Players Club in Vegas, is that clubs offer tiers, status levels which once attained offer higher value benefits. As your level of play increases, so do the benefits! Once you've attained a higher status or tier level at one casino, some competitor casinos offer a tier matching promotion or loss rebate for new sign-ups! If you've already earned a higher status at one casino, or acquired Mlife Pearl Status or Total Rewards Platinum Status through the previously mentioned casino credit card promotional offers, take advantage of competitors tier matching promotions!

In closing this section it is important to dispel a few common myths. The player tracking system into which you insert your Players Card on Video Poker, Video Keno and Slot machines, is completely separate from the gaming program. Like a meter, the tracking system records coins-in and coins-out only, it is in no way connected with game play! Regardless of whether you insert a Players Card or not, the outcome of the game would be the same! And don't worry, casinos do not share this data with the IRS!

SLOTS

A Slot machine pays out less money than it takes in. In Nevada (for each gaming jurisdiction can have different regulations) the minimum payout amount is regulated at 75%, but actual payout percentages are higher. As was shown earlier, the average in Nevada is roughly 93%. A Random Number Generator chip (RNG) controls the payback percentage for a single machine, and to change a machines percentage, a new chip must be purchased from the games manufacturer then installed. Over time, which is how gaming percentages are calculated, no machine will pay out more than it takes in!

♠♥♣♦

VIDEO POKER

The main difference between Video Poker and Slots is that a Slot machine is a game of luck, and Video Poker is a game of skill. When playing a Slot machine, even an interactive version, there is no decision that can affect the outcome. In Video Poker on the other hand, your skill in playing the cards affects the outcome.

To put some common misconceptions about video poker to rest, in Nevada a Video Poker game is played with a standard 52 card deck. Jokers Wild variants of course, also utilize jokers. Multiple-line variants utilize one deck per line. Therefore, a three-line game would use three separate decks of cards. When not in play, a RNG is constantly shuffling the 2,598,960 possible hand combinations. The cards are dealt in the serial manner, which means when you hit the deal or max bet button, your first five cards are determined and dealt off the top of the deck. After you hold whichever cards you desire for your hand, the next five cards are determined at the time the draw button is pressed.

Unlike Slot machines, every Video Poker machine's payback percentage can be mathematically calculated and easily determined by the payout table on the machine. A Video Poker machine cannot be "tightened" as many suggest, without changing the program and payout table displayed on the machine. You can always determine what the payback percentage is on any given machine prior to play. (Payback percentages are based on perfect play over millions of hands.)

♠♥♣♦

There is also a chance; regardless of percentages, knowledge of a game and strategic play; that plain old dumb luck will determine whether you win or lose!

Many years ago I was playing quarter Full Pay Deuces Wild at the Fiesta Henderson, when a petite elderly lady sat down on the end machine next to me and inserted a twenty dollar bill into the validator. About fifteen minutes later, out of the corner of my eye I noticed that the lady had been dealt three deuces, an ace and a seven. To my astonishment, the lady held the three deuces and the ace, a major error when dealt three deuces! Before I could assist her by suggesting to only hold the deuces, which mathematically would increase her chance of drawing the fourth, she hit the draw button and out popped the fourth deuce! The lady was so excited she turned to me and exclaimed: "I've got five Aces!" . . . to which I responded . . . "Ma'am, I am sure the casino would be happy to pay you $18.75 for five-of-a-kind, but you actually have four deuces which pays $250!"

Having luck in Video Poker also means you can hold all the wrong cards every hand, and still be a winner! I'll never forget sitting next a gentleman playing Triple Deuces at Boulder Station, whom was holding the wrong cards on almost every hand! A person's play is of course none of my business, but you hate seeing people throw money away by making wrong decisions, thereby increasing the casinos edge. Even so, I held my tongue. Then I looked over and the gentlemen had held just a ten of spades! No matter what Video Poker game you're playing (other than a tens or better game), there should never be a reason to hold a solitary ten! As I was contemplating whether I would say something or not, the gentleman hit the draw button. You guessed it . . . out popped the Ace, King, Queen and Jack of Spades for a Royal Flush!

In gaming you can be lucky, but luck is short lived. Poor play, making errors that could be avoided, generates casino profits and breaks many a player. The reality is that in any game of chance knowledge is power. To increase your odds of winning or breaking even (also considered a win by many) it is necessary that prior to your first wager you learn basic game strategy.

The biggest mistake novice Video Poker players make (which greatly affects the house edge), is not playing maximum coins. Video Poker machines pay a bonus for a Natural Royal Flush (no wild cards) when 5 coins are bet. If you bet 1 to 4 coins the payout is 250 coins for each coin bet. With a maximum 5 coin bet, a Natural Royal Flush pays 800 coins for each coin bet! If you're going to play Video Poker, always play 5 coins!

TIP: If you feel uncomfortable playing maximum bet at a certain denomination, or cannot afford to play max bet on a given denomination, play maximum coins at a lower denomination machine!

♠♥♣♦

Numerous variations of Video Poker are offered in Nevada casinos. Common games include • **Jacks or Better** • **Bonus Poker** • **Double Bonus** • **Double Double Bonus** • **Triple Bonus** • **Bonus Poker Deluxe** • **Super Aces Bonus** • **Jokers Wild** • **Deuces Wild** • **Triple Pay Deuces Wild** • **Loose Deuces** • **Deuces Wild Bonus** •

Not only does each Video Poker game variation require a different strategy of play, but different pay tables exist for each game variation! Jacks or Better for example, has more than twenty payout schedules available and the strategy for one pay table could be disastrous to your bankroll if used playing another! Here is a sampling of some pay tables and theoretical returns for the more common **Jacks or Better** and **Deuces Wild Video Poker** games:

JACKS OR BETTER VIDEO POKER

The payout numbers represent payout per coin bet for each of the following winning poker hands: Royal Flush • Straight Flush • 4 Of-a-Kind • Full House • Flush • Straight • 3 Of-a-Kind • Two Pair • One Pair Jacks or Better • Theoretical return percentages are calculated based on <u>maximum coin bet</u> and perfect strategy play. The name of each game variant refers to the Full House/Straight payouts.

800•50•25•**9**•**6**•4•3•2•1• Known as **9/6 Jacks or Better**, this pay table results in a 99.54% theoretical return!

800•50•25•**9**•**5**•4•3•2•1• Known as **9/5 Jacks or Better**, this pay table results in a 98.45% theoretical return.

800•50•25•**8**•**6**•4•3•2•1• Known as **8/6 Jacks or Better**, this pay table results in a 98.39% theoretical return.

800•50•25•**8**•**5**•4•3•2•1 Known as **8/5 Jacks or Better**, this pay table results in a 97.28% theoretical return.

800•50•25•**7**•**5**•4•3•2•1• Known as **7/5 Jacks or Better**, this pay table results in a 96.15% theoretical return.

800•50•25•**6**•**5**•4•3•2•1• Known as **6/5 Jacks or Better**, this pay table results in a 95% theoretical return.

♠♥♣♦

DEUCES WILD VIDEO POKER

The payout numbers represent payout per coin bet for each of the following winning poker hands: Natural Royal Flush • 4 Deuces • Wild Royal Flush • 5 Of-a-Kind • Straight Flush • 4 Of-a-Kind • Full House • Flush • Straight • 3 Of-a-Kind • Theoretical return percentages are calculated based on <u>maximum coin bet</u> and perfect strategy play.

800•200•25•15•9•5•3•2•2•1• Known as **Full Pay Deuces Wild**, this pay table results in a 100.76% theoretical return!

800•200•20•12•9•5•3•2•2•1• Known as **Pseudo Full Pay Deuces Wild**, this pay table results in a 98.94% theoretical return.

800•200•25•16•10•4•4•3•2•1• Known as **NSU (not-so-ugly) Deuces Wild**, this pay table results in a 99.73% theoretical return.

800•200•25•15•9•4•4•3•2•1• Known as **Pseudo NSU Deuces Wild**, This pay table results in a 98.91% theoretical return.

800•200•20•12•10•4•4•3•2•1• Deuces Wild pay table results in a 97.58% theoretical return.

800•200•25•16•13•4•3•2•2•1• Deuces Wild pay table results in a 96.77% theoretical return.

800•200•20•10•8•4•4•3•2•1• Deuces Wild pay table results in a 95.96% theoretical return.

800•200•20•10•8•4•4•3•2•1• Deuces Wild pay table results in a 95.96% theoretical return.

800•200•25•15•10•4•3•2•2•1• Deuces Wild pay table results in a 94.82% theoretical return.

The **Deuces Deluxe** game variation has two additional winning hand combinations; a Natural 4-Of-a-Kind (pays 10 coins) and a Natural Straight Flush (pays 50 coins). This games pay table results in a 100.34% theoretical return!

800•200•50•25•15•10•9•4•4•3•2•1•

♠♥♣♦

The preceding examples of Video Poker pay tables clearly show how a casino, by changing the payout on just two winning hands, can increase the house edge. But if you choose the machine you play on wisely, the player can have an advantage, not the casino! As can be seen, on Full Pay Deuces Wild the player has the advantage at 100.76%! The theoretical return also increases when the basic value of Players Club base, bonus and multiple points are calculated!

For this reason, my personal games of choice are Full Pay and NSU Deuces Wild. In addition to game strategy being fairly easy to learn, and the games being fun to play, by choosing to play variations with better pay tables, the player has the edge not the casino!

♠♥♣♦

TABLE GAMES

Las Vegas casinos offer numerous games of chance in addition to Slot, Video Poker and Keno machines. Casinos that offer Bingo have a room separated from the casino, many times located on the second floor. Live keno can be found in the majority of casinos. You can play in the keno room (typically near the Sports Book) or throughout the casino by placing your wager with a keno girl or keno runner (the girl walking around the casino and restaurants calling out "keno"…"keno"). Casinos that offer Live Poker Games typically have a separate Poker Room, although some smaller casinos provide tables in the Pit area. The Pit of a casino is where you will find all other Table Games, except of course the "high limit" room, typically not where you'd expect to find the frugal gambler!

♠♥♣♦

Table Poker

Live poker (or table poker) is where the casino provides a table, the cards and a dealer, but you are playing against other players, not the casino. The casino edge on this game is the rake, a certain percentage (with a cap) taken from every pot. Made popular by the World Series of Poker and internet gambling sites, live poker is still very popular, but with the death of internet poker since the government crackdown, Las Vegas has seen a steady trend of poker room downsizing and closures. The good news for the poker enthusiast is that live poker can still be found at nearly forty casinos, either in a room by itself or near the Pit.

The most common games offered in Vegas are limit and no-limit Texas Hold'em, Omaha and Stud Poker. Almost all poker rooms have daily Tournaments and some even offer Freeroll Tournament promotions. There are great online resources available to locate poker rooms and games in the Las Vegas valley. To see complete details; including minimum buy-ins, rake, comp info and promotions visit: **www.pokeratlas.com/las-vegas-nevada**

Some casinos even offer live, real-time poker room information online! The Wynn provides tournament information, games in progress and waiting list information online at: **www.wynnpoker.com**

Red Rock Resorts provides real-time poker room information online for Red Rock, Green Valley Ranch, Santa Fe Station, Boulder Station and Palace Station at: **www.stationcasinospoker.com**

♠♥♣♦

Generally, the games offered in the Pit area of a casino are Blackjack, Roulette (typically double zero American layout, but some also offer European single zero layout), Craps, Baccarat, Mini-Baccarat, Pai Gow, 3-Card Poker, Let-It-Ride, Caribbean Stud and the Big Six Wheel. The games, variations and odds offered can differ from casino to casino, as well as by location (Strip, Downtown, Off-Strip). Keep in mind that <u>every</u> game of chance in a casino has a built in house advantage or "edge," which is attained by paying out less than the games true odds.

♠♥♣♦

Blackjack

Blackjack is by far the most popular casino Table Game. The house edge in Blackjack varies by casino and game variant. The following factors affect the house advantage; number of decks of cards used, dealer hits or stands on soft 17; player can double after a split; player can double on any first two cards, 9-11 only or 10-11 only; player can re-split to 2, 3 or 4 hands; player can re-split Aces; player can hit split Aces; player loses only original bet against dealer Blackjack; surrender rule; and whether a Blackjack pays 3 to 2 (a $10 bet would pay $15) or 6 to 5 (a $10 bet would pay $12).

Rule changes are where a casino increases the house edge. Normally a Blackjack pays 3 to 2, but when a casino changes the payout to 6 to 5 the house edge increases by 1.40%! Even worse, a Blackjack payout of 1 to 1 increases the house edge by 2.30%! A Dealer hitting a soft 17 increases the house edge by .20%. The number of decks being dealt also greatly effects the house edge. A two deck game increases the house advantage by .32%, four decks by .49%, six decks by .54% and eight decks by .57%!

If you can find them, tables with rules that benefit the player (reduce the house edge) allow a double after split, late surrender, re-split Aces and/or double down anytime.

TIP: Only play on Blackjack tables that offer a 3 to 2 payout for a Blackjack and a game dealt with as few decks as possible! Learn basic game strategy; when to hit, stand, split, double and surrender.

There is a nice online survey published in January 2016 that compares 3/2 Blackjack games, their rules and house edges offered by each specific Vegas casino. The lowest house edge is .25532%, the highest 2.82051%. Check the survey out at: **www.wizardofvegas.com/guides/blackjack-survey/**

As in Video Poker, poor play increases the house advantage. The more skillful you play, the lower the house advantage. For example, whether single or multiple deck, basic strategy rules are to never split 10s and always stand on hard 17. Should you break these rules and other basic strategies, you'll increase the house edge even more.

TIP: When playing keep in mind some simple mathematical facts. The dealer will bust more often when his up card is a 2 (35%), 3 (38%), 4 (40%), 5 (43%) or 6 (42%). The dealer will complete more hands when his up card is a 7 (26%), 8 (24%), 9 (23%), 10 (21%) or Ace (11%). (Percentages represent the chance the dealer's up card will bust)

♠♥♣♦

Roulette

On American layout Roulette, mathematically the house advantage is 5.26% on every possible bet (except the 5-number bet { 0, 00, 1, 2, 3 } which is 7.89%). Put simply, day in and day out a casino expects to win 5.26% of all money wagered in Roulette! The longer you play, the house edge will eat away at your bankroll! To beat any house edge you must get lucky, win quickly and cash out!

The European layout version of roulette with only single 0, offers better odds than the American version. With only one zero, the house edge drops to 2.70% on every bet! These games are usually found in higher end casinos and require higher minimum bets. By the way, have you ever noticed that the sum of all numbers on a roulette layout equals the popular culture sign of the devil . . . 666!

♠♥♣♦

In any game of chance knowledge is power. Just as was the case for Video Poker, to reduce the house edge and enhance your odds of winning or breaking even, it is necessary that prior to your first wager you learn basic game strategy!

For the beginner or novice player, many casinos provide an opportunity to learn the fundamentals that are unique to each game, through FREE lessons. Usually a sign on an empty table in the Pit area indicates which games, and at what times, lessons are being offered. If not, ask in the Pit if any lessons are being offered at that casino.

♠♥♣♦

WIN CARDS®
Gaming International, Inc.
www.wincards.com
• 775.588.4222 • Toll Free 866.4 wincards •

P a g e | **143**

Another way to learn to play Blackjack, Craps and Roulette, is through the use of **WIN CARDS**®, a promotional product sold through casinos that includes non-negotiable gaming chips. WIN CARDS® are available at the Players Club or Main Cashier. Currently available at:

• **Circus Circus** • **Four Queens** • **Tropicana** •
• **Mandalay Bay** • **Railroad Pass** •

Dependent on the casino, when you purchase a set of three WIN CARDS® for $10, you will also receive $15 in non-negotiable casino chips, or, when you purchase a set of three WIN CARDS® for $20 you will also receive $30 in non-negotiable chips.

• **Blackjack Win Card**® •

Shows possible hit, stand, double down and split options for the blackjack beginner.

• **Craps Win Card**® •

Shows the exact odds for Pass and Don't Pass, Come and Don't Come, as well as Place Bets. Use it to help follow the table action.

• **Roulette Win Card**® •

Shows the payoffs for three common bets: Straight Up (on a number), Split (between two numbers) and Corner Bets (split between four numbers).

♠♥♣♦

The IRS & Gaming

Nevada has no state income tax. Should you hit a Bingo or Slot device jackpot (Slots, Video Poker, Video Keno) of $1,200 or more $1,500 or more from live Keno, it is considered a reportable jackpot for federal income tax purposes. Winnings from Table Games (except for wins of over 300 to 1 and for Poker Tournament winnings over $5,000) are typically not reportable.

If you are a US Resident (or Non Resident with an individual taxpayer identification number "ITIN") the Internal Revenue Service requires that the casino report the jackpot on IRS Form W2G. Tax withholding is not required if you provide the casino with your Social Security number (your card or a Form W9). However, you do have the little known option of requesting withholding by the casino for any amount. If you do not provide the casino with a Social Security number, the jackpot will be subject to 28% withholding, which will offset taxes owed or be refunded when you file your Federal Income Tax Return.

Non-Residents that cannot provide an ITIN are subject to 30% withholding. (To obtain an ITIN file IRS Form W-7 *Application for IRS Individual Taxpayer Identification Number* with the Internal Revenue Service.)

TIP: Non-Residents from certain countries may be exempt from the 30% withholding requirement due to International Tax Treaties between their country and the United States. If you are a resident from a country exempted by treaty, in order to claim the exemption and avoid withholding you will need to supply the casino with IRS Form W-8BEN prior to the jackpot being paid. Once supplied to the casino, the form is valid for a period of three years.

If you do not provide the casino with the appropriate form and money is withheld from your jackpot payout, you will need to file a US Non-Resident Tax Return to get the amount withheld refunded by the IRS. Check the following Internal Revenue Service publications and forms for more information:

www.irs.gov/pub/irs-pdf/fw7.pdf

www.irs.gov/uac/publication-515-withholding-of-tax-on-nonresident-aliens-and-foreign-entities

www.irs.gov/pub/irs-pdf/fw8ben.pdf

TIP: Previously I've indicated that you need not worry, the casino doesn't share player tracking data with the Internal Revenue Service. Actually, casinos will share this data with the IRS, but only upon your request. At your request, Players Clubs will provide you with a *Year-end Win-loss Record* of your play at that particular casino for the year, which can be used to help offset your wins with losses for tax purposes!

♠♥♣♦

FREE THINGS TO DO

♠♥♣♦

Many years ago I came to the conclusion that nothing in life is free. Everything we consume, come in contact with, or do, has an inherent cost or value, whether large or small. "Free water," someone has paid for the power to pump, filter and bottle; "free parking," whether in a lot or garage, someone paid to build and maintain; "free phone calls," have a cost to the customer and provider; a "free gift with purchase," was manufactured, purchased and comes with strings attached; a "B1G1 offer," is actually a 50% discount; taking a shower, using the rest room, hitchhiking, in short everything has some hidden cost that someone must pay.

My first born child couldn't have been more than four years old when I attempted to explain this concept. As a proud parent I thought I was being prophetic passing on what one day would become an invaluable concept. After a few moments my daughter responded . . . "I know something that is free daddy!" Chuckling to myself I said . . . "Oh really! And what might that be?" With her reply I was speechless. There was no possible way I could contradict her reasoning. "Daddy" she said . . . "everything we get from Santa Claus is free!"

At that point in my life I hadn't visited Vegas yet. Although I still believe in the concept that nothing is free in life, many things, especially in Vegas, can appear free! As a matter of fact, there is so much to do and see in Vegas that you will not be able to cram everything into one short visit. What follows are many things to do in Vegas . . . at no cost to you!

♠♥♣♦

If you are arriving in Vegas through McCarran International Airport, you'll probably be in a rush to get to your hotel and hit the casino. You will probably walk right by the free **Howard W. Cannon Aviation Museum** exhibits. But on your way out of town, you might wish to visit the main exhibit on Level 2 above baggage claim in Terminal 1. Other exhibits are located in the gate areas, ticketing, and along the moving walkway in the C Gate area.

Having flown into Vegas, you've obviously missed the iconic **Welcome to Fabulous Las Vegas Sign** described earlier in the *Welcome to Las Vegas* chapter. Well worth a visit for an iconic photo opportunity!

Las Vegas Boulevard in itself is a sightseeing marvel. Take in the sights with a slow journey along the Strip by car, bus, tram or foot, but remember distances can be deceiving and keep hydrated with plenty of water. The elevated pedestrian cross walks offer great vistas and photo opportunities.

♠♥♣♦

Once on the Strip you'll want to visit another iconic Vegas attraction, **The Volcano at the Mirage,** set in a lagoon with palm trees and cascading waterfalls at the front of the hotel. The volcano's sensational eruption, spitting fire 60 feet into the air, is choreographed to a soundtrack composed by Grateful Dead drummer Mickey Hart and Zakir Hussain. The volcano comes to life nightly at 8 PM & 9 PM, with an additional show on Friday & Saturday nights at 10 PM.

Down the street at Bellagio, the 8.5 acre lake that is home to the iconic **Fountains of Bellagio** comes to life with a dazzling spectacle of water, music and light Monday through Friday from 3 PM to 8 PM every 30 minutes, then every 15 minutes until midnight. On Saturdays and Holidays the fountains come to life earlier at noon. On Sundays the shows begin at 11 AM running every 30 minutes until 7 PM, then every 15 minutes until midnight.

After taking in the spectacle outside, stroll inside Bellagio and be awed by the sights within. The vibrant **Dale Chihuly Glass Sculpture** *Fiori Di Como* hangs majestically above the lobby. Two thousand colorful hand-blown glass blossoms, weighing about 40,000 pounds, cover 2,100 square feet of the lobby ceiling!

Located just past the lobby is the **Bellagio Conservatory & Botanical Gardens**. This 90,000 square-foot glass domed conservatory features a 14,000 square-foot seasonal floral

showcase. Displays for the balance of 2017 are:
- *Summer Garden Show* May 27 to September 9 •
- *Harvest Show* from September 16 to November 25 •
- *Holiday Show* from December 2 to January 6 •

The conservatory is DARK while setting up between shows.
www.bellagio.com/en/entertainment/conservatory-botanical-garden.html

While at Bellagio take the opportunity to drop by the **Chocolate Fountain in Bellagio** located at the Jean-Philippe Patisserie. The world's largest chocolate fountain, it stands 27 feet tall and circulates more than 2,100 pounds of melted dark, milk and white chocolate through 500 feet of pipes 24 hours a day year-round!

Cirque du Soleil presents **The Art of Richard MacDonald**, an exhibition showcasing over 50 bronze sculptures, drawings, serigraphs and lithographs. Located in the "O" Theater Lobby at Bellagio, which is open from 10 AM to 11 PM Monday & Tuesday, 10 AM to 1 AM Wednesday through Sunday.

Hop on the free tram from Bellagio (described in the *Transportation* chapter) to Crystals in CityCenter, the home to a second gallery of **The Art of Richard MacDonald**. A 40 foot waterfall, split face stone walls and curved steel provide a backdrop to over 50 pieces of bronze sculpture, drawings and paintings by the artist. 10 AM to 11 PM Sunday through Thursday, until midnight on Friday & Saturday.

While at CityCenter you can also view the **CityCenter Fine Art Collection**. The collection consists of almost two dozen works from acclaimed artists, and is on display throughout CityCenter (mainly at Aria). The collection is accessible to the public and free to view. A downloadable map and guide to the collection is available at:
www.aria.com/en/amenities/aria-fine-art-collection.html

It is Free to visit the **Barrick Museum** located on the **University of Nevada Las Vegas** campus, but they "suggest" a voluntary contribution of $5 for adults, $2 for seniors. Open Monday through Friday 8 AM to 5 PM;

Thursdays until 8 PM; Saturday 12 PM to 5 PM. Offers a variety of exhibits and collections. Visit their website for more details: **www.unlv.edu/barrickmuseum/collections**

♠♥♣♦

The Lake of Dreams at Wynn Las Vegas, with its 40-foot waterfall and pine-topped mountain, offers a spectacular show of light, water, music and imagery every half hour from dusk until 11:30 PM nightly.

While at the Wynn, don't miss the **Jeff Koons Sculpture** *Popeye*, crafted of chromium stainless steel with a vibrant color coating. *Popeye* was purchased in 2014 by Steve Wynn for $28.2 million. Wynn reportedly turned down a $40 to $60 million offer from a rival collector just a year later (amount varies dependent on the source)! *Popeye* is destined to leave Las Vegas for its future home at Wynn Boston Harbor in Everett, Massachusetts, slated to be opening in June 2019.

Advertised as a "serene paradise," the 15-acre **Flamingo Wildlife Habitat** is stocked with a collection of exotic birds (a flock of Chilean flamingos, swans, pelicans, and ibis), fish and turtles, on public display from 8 AM till dusk. Pelican feedings are 8:30 AM & 2 PM daily!

Across the street from the Flamingo at the Forum Shops in Caesars Palace is the **Fall of Atlantis**, a 7 minute animatronic giant talking statue fountain show that plays daily on the hour from 11 AM. Surrounding the base of the fountain is the 50,000 gallon saltwater **Atlantis Aquarium**. Daily feedings are 1:15 PM and 5:15 PM.

Further up the Strip you won't want to miss the **Palazzo Atrium** located at the entrance to the Grand Canal Shoppes. This multi-story atrium features a two-story waterfall, domed skylight, and seasonal exotic flower displays. While in the neighborhood, take a leisurely stroll through the Venetian streetscape and be entertained by costumed street performers at the Grand Canal Shoppes and **Venetian Gondola Canals**!

Miracle Mile Shops Fountain, located in front of the "V" Theater at Planet Hollywood Resort & Casino, features lighted water effects, eruptions and color changing fog choreographed to music. Shows are daily at the top of the hour from noon to 11 PM.

The Grand Bazaar Shops **Canopy Light Show** at Bally's, lights up the night to themed soundtracks every 15 minutes from 8:05 PM daily. And high above the Swarovski store the **Swarovski Starburst**, a giant starburst made up of more than 900 crystals, illuminates the night sky at 9 PM and midnight daily.

For the Rock Stars among us, visit the **Memorabilia and Rock Wall** at Hard Rock Café on Las Vegas Boulevard. This interactive touch wall (18 feet wide by 4 foot tall) of the brand's music memorabilia collection is free to view from 11 AM to 1 AM daily, until 2 AM on Friday & Saturday.

Two long blocks east from the Strip on Harmon Avenue (1.3 mile walk, no city bus on Harmon), a display of **Rock 'n' Roll Memorabilia** adorns the walls of the Hard Rock Hotel. Free to view 24 hours a day**.**

♠♥♣♦

Mystic Falls Park is a 25,000 square foot indoor park located by registration in the center of Sam's Town Casino. The free **Sunset Stampede Laser Light and Water Show** is presented daily at 2 PM, 4 PM, 6 PM, 8 PM & 10 PM. From the Strip take the free Sam's Town Shuttle from Harrah's, or eastbound RTC Flamingo 202; from Downtown take the free Sam's Town Shuttle from the Fremont, or southbound RTC Boulder Highway Express (BHX).

For the kid in all of us, the **Carnival Midway** at Circus Circus surrounds a circus stage that showcases free circus acts daily from 11 AM.

♠♥♣♦

Having been tantalized by the chocolate fountain at Bellagio, you'll be pleased to know that Vegas doesn't disappoint when it comes to the chocolate lover in all of us! The main attraction of **Hershey's Chocolate World** at New York-New York Hotel & Casino, is a sculpture of the Statue of Liberty made out of nearly 800 pounds of milk chocolate! Apart from the sculpture, this is a retail store with Hershey gift items, chocolates, candies, and a mouth-watering selection of baked goods. The store is open 9 AM to 11 PM daily, except Friday & Saturday when it stays open until midnight.

Another chocolate retail outlet, **M & M's World Las Vegas**, specializes in M&M's candy and merchandise. Located just across the street in the Showcase Mall next to the MGM Grand, the free attractions offered consist of a display wall of M & M's in almost every color, a replica of the M & M's NASCAR race car, and a 3D theater that shows the movie short *I Lost My M In Vegas*, starring Red and Yellow. Store is open daily 9 AM to midnight. The 3D movie plays until 8 PM on Saturdays, Sundays & Mondays, and until 6 PM Tuesdays, Wednesdays & Thursdays.

M & M's World Henderson is a small retail shop at the entrance to the **Ethel M Chocolates Factory** self-guided tour (viewing aisle). To celebrate the 35th Anniversary of Ethel M Chocolates, the self-guided viewing aisle and the chocolate shop have been completely remodeled. The redesigned self-guided tours are free and open to the public. The tour terminates in the Ethel M Chocolates retail outlet, where you are provided a free sample.

Adjacent to the Ethel M factory is the 3-acre **Botanical Cactus Garden** featuring over 300 types of cactus, where you can take a leisurely stroll. If you are visiting around the holidays, don't miss the dazzling display of the gardens decked out in Christmas tree lights! Open every day from 8:30 AM to 10 PM. Ethel M's is a bit of a drive from the Strip, but can be reached by taking RTC bus route **212 Sunset** eastbound from the South Strip Transfer Terminal.

If you thought Ethel M's Factory was small, visit **Hexx Chocolate & Confections,** a premium chocolatier located at the Paris Casino Resort that creates five unique chocolate flavors on site in their chocolate kitchen, from "bean to bar." Hexx has a chocolate and candy retail shop with an ice cream counter and the entire process can be viewed from a "tasting counter" where the chocolate flavors are sampled. PAYING FOR A TOUR IS NOT RECOMMENDED.

♠♥♣♦

Water, water, everywhere! Except in Lake Mead which is at its lowest point since 1937 when it was first filled! It's hard to remember you're in the middle of the desert! One of the last attractions you'd expect to encounter in a desert environment is an aquarium, but they seem to appear everywhere you look! The wall behind hotel registration at the Mirage is home to the 53 foot long, 20,000 gallon **Coral Reef Aquarium** and its 60 species of coral reef inhabitants! You don't need to check-in, to check-out this free attraction! The Mirage is also home of the **Tropical Rain Forest Atrium**, located just inside the front entrance under a 100-foot high dome. Here you can enjoy the tranquility amongst the lagoons, waterfall, palm trees, orchids and bromelaids!

Further south but off-Strip is **The Aquarium** at Silverton. This 117,000 gallon saltwater tank is home to over 4,000 tropical fish, stingrays, sharks and the occasional mermaid. Interactive feedings are daily at 1:30 PM & 4:30 PM. Mermaid swims are held three times a day Thursday through Sunday. Current hours available online at: **www.silvertoncasino.com/amenities/aquarium/**

If you've never visited the **Bass Pro Shops** at Silverton, check out the numerous taxidermy displays throughout this massive store. Bass Pro Shops is also home to an 18,000 gallon water feature that simulates Red Rock Canyon's rock formation, and three additional freshwater aquariums that feature trout, channel catfish, carp, and of course, bass.

If you plan on visiting Las Vegas next year during tax season, one paid attraction actually makes the list of free things to do! Usually, a promotion is run where a temporary U.S. Mail location is established at **The Shark Reef** at Mandalay Bay where you can post your Federal Tax Return. In exchange, you get free admission to the 1.3 million gallon aquarium! In April 2017 call 702.632.7777 to check on availability.

♠♥♣♦

Not to be outdone, Downtown Vegas has its share of free attractions and aquariums! The **Chart House Aquarium** located in full view behind registration at Golden Nugget, is a 75,000 gallon tropical fish aquarium. The unique 200,000 gallon **Shark Aquarium** at Golden Nugget has the hotels 3-story pool water slide (The Tank) running through it!

While visiting the Golden Nugget, where else would you expect to view the world's largest gold nugget? The *Hand of Faith* gold nugget was found in 1980 in Australia and weighs almost 62 pounds! The Golden Nugget Hotel purchased the nugget for a million dollars and has it on public display 24 hours a day.

The **Fremont Street Experience** is probably the widest known free attraction Downtown, if not in all Las Vegas! This five block entertainment district and pedestrian mall, is best known for the **Viva Vision Light Show**. Viva Vision is the world's largest video screen (1500 foot long, 90 feet wide and suspended 90 feet above the pedestrian mall). The VivaVision screen features a free light show every night of the week from 8 PM to 1 AM, every hour on the hour. Each hour features a different show, so stick around awhile! Fremont Street Experience is frequented by a diverse variety of street entertainers, and provides access to casinos, restaurants, bars, shops and retail kiosks. The Experience also hosts live concerts and entertainment on its three stages.

Binion's Gambling Hall on Fremont Street Experience is home to a **$1,000,000 Display**. The display contains one million dollars in denominations from ones to hundred dollar bills. If you are 21 or older, Binion's will take a free souvenir photo of you with the display from 9 AM to 11:30 PM daily.

At the Las Vegas Boulevard end (east) of the Fremont Street Experience, inside the Neonopolis Complex, discover the small micro-brewery **Banger Brewing**. Open Sunday through Thursday from noon to midnight, Friday & Saturday from noon to 1 AM. Banger Brewing offers free guided tours daily, you must be 21 or older and space is limited to 8 people per tour. For dates, times and to sign-up online, visit: **www.bangerbrewing.com/tours/**

Just a block from Fremont Street Experience, a unique collection of antiques is on display at **Main Street Station Hotel Casino & Brewery**. From the Plaza, stroll north along Main Street on the promenade to Main Street Station. On public view inside, the antique collection includes stained glass, bronze doors, chandeliers, a wild boar bronzed statue, a portion of the Berlin Wall (displayed in the men's room of all places), and many more. A brochure and guide to the collection is available at the Main Street Station Front and Bell Desks, or online at **http://vegasexperience.com/wp-content/uploads/2015/04/main-street-antique-guide.pdf**

The Golden Gate, the oldest casino in Las Vegas, has a small but interesting collection of memorabilia from the era when the hotel was the Hotel Nevada and Sal Sagev (Las Vegas spelled backwards) located in a built-in display case between the Players Club desk and hotel registration.

The El Cortez, a short walk from Fremont Street Experience, is home to **Jackie Gaughan's Downtown Las Vegas Exhibit**, a modest exhibit of casino chips, tokens, dice, cards, shot glasses and other memorabilia. Being displayed in three showcases across from the El Cortez Players Club counter, the exhibit is available to view 24 hours a day.

At 707 East Fremont Street is the **Downtown Container Park**, an open air shopping center that features the interactive play area **Children's Tree House & Slide**, a selection of retail stores, restaurants, and nightlife. For a current events schedule visit: **http://downtowncontainerpark.com/events/month/**

While visiting Downtown you might want to learn about the art, architecture and history of The Smith Center for the Performing Arts campus. Free sixty minute **Guided Walking Tours** are offered but limited to twenty patrons. Check dates & availability online. Tours must be booked online. **www.thesmithcenter.com/your-visit/public-tours/**

♠♥♣♦

When leaving Downtown, stop in and check out the **Gold and Silver Pawn Shop** of History Channel fame! Who knows, you might even get to rub elbows with the Pawn Stars themselves ("the Old Man," Rick Harrison, Corey or Chumlee). Have a good look around, but don't expect to find anything else free here. Not just a pawn shop, assorted show souvenirs are also available.

Located at 713 South Las Vegas Boulevard, the Pawn Shop is not directly serviced by a city bus route. Take the Strip & Downtown Express (SDX) or the Deuce on the Strip northbound to the Bonneville Transit Center (BTC). From the BTC the Pawn Shop is a 3 block walk eastbound on Garces Avenue. Or, board the southbound Deuce at Bay 19 of the BTC which has a stop on Las Vegas Boulevard just south of the Pawn Shop.

♠♥♣♦

CBS Television City at the MGM Grand is a consumer research facility offering focus groups, one-on-one interviews and surveys to clients in all industries. If you've got some spare time, stop by and see about participating in a screening or survey. Not only is it free, they sometimes offer incentives for helping out! Open daily from 10 AM to 8:30 PM, screenings every 30 minutes. **www.tvcityresearch.com**

Another research facility, **The Preview Center**, is located in Bally's Avenue Shops, just down the escalator from Bally's casino floor. Preview new show pilots and rate them before the public. It's free and they give you from $10 to $25 for your time and opinion. Preview takes from 40 minutes up to 2 hours. Days of operation and hours vary.

Mystère at the TI (Treasure Island) is advertising free open rehearsals on Mondays at 4 PM. All ages are admitted for the half hour rehearsal of these amazing athletes & dancers. Open rehearsal offers come and go, so please double check to verify they are listed on the website before you go. **http://www.treasureisland.com/shows/2/mystere-by-cirque-du-soleil**

TIP: Occasionally the **Tournament of Kings** at Excalibur invites everyone to "Journey to medieval times and get a behind-the-scenes glimpse of how the show is produced." When open rehearsals are available they are listed on: **www.excalibur.com/en/entertainment/tournament-of-kings.html**.

TIP: Free open rehearsals for **The Beatles Love** Cirque du Soleil show at the Mirage also come and go. When available, guests are invited to "Watch artists do what they do best - flips, twists, and jumps! Cirque du Soleil invites the public to come watch artists rehearse acts from the show." When open rehearsals are available they are listed on: **https://www.mirage.com/en/entertainment/the-beatles-love.html**

Stop by the Rio and enjoy free one-of-a-kind "**BevErtainment**," where "**BevErtainers**" not only serve cocktails, but sing and dance on five stages throughout the casino. The last show of the iconic Masquerade in the Sky was in February 2013, but the **Masquerade Village at the Rio** offers live music Friday, Saturday and select Thursdays from 9 PM to 12 AM. For the current schedule visit: **https://www.caesars.com/rio-las-vegas/things-to-do/masquerade-bar#.WBNeoNQrKt9**

♠♥♣♦

For those with their own transportation, there are also many free things to do on the outskirts of Las Vegas. The better known tourist and recreational sites include: **Clark County Wetlands Park**, **Red Rock Canyon Visitor Center**, **Mount Charleston**, **Lake Mead**, **Hoover Dam** and the **Mike O'Callaghan-Pat Tillman Memorial Bridge**, the world's highest concrete arch bridge. There is also another, yet temporary, man-made wonder in the desert:

Seven Magic Mountains, a public art installation of Swiss artist Ugo Rondinone, is located in the desert outside of Las Vegas. *Seven Magic Mountains* features seven thirty to thirty-five-foot high day glow totems comprised of painted, locally-sourced boulders. Visible across the desert landscape along Interstate 15 *Seven Magic Mountains* is approximately

10 miles south of the intersection of Las Vegas Boulevard and St. Rose Parkway in Henderson. The exhibition opened May 11, 2016 and will be on view for just two years. From Las Vegas follow I-15 south to Sloan Road (exit 25); turn left (east) to Las Vegas Boulevard; turn right and drive approximately 7 miles south; the artwork will appear on your left (east). **www.sevenmagicmountains.com**

Can't make it out to the *Seven Magic Mountains* desert site? A miniature model of the exhibit is on display near the Monte Carlo & Aria Tram Station/self-parking. From the Aria self-park lobby take the escalator up, display case is in the wall straight ahead at the top of the escalator. From the Monte Carlo take the "Street of Dreams" (shops and restaurants are closed but access walkway is open during construction) toward the Tram Station. At the top of escalator go straight instead of turning left to Tram Station, display is just through the doors on the right.

Free Wi-Fi

Internet access has become a necessary amenity for today's tech-savvy travelers. In Vegas there are many options available to stay connected. Most properties provide internet access in their rooms for a fee (included in the resort fee) and also in their business center (either included in resort fee or as a pay-for-use service). Some properties even provide non-guests the option to purchase hourly or daily internet access via credit card, or provide pay-for-use internet kiosks (typically located near the hotel lobby).

Regardless, the most sought-after freebie in Las Vegas is probably free Wi-Fi. Connecting to the internet in Vegas for free is not as hard as it may initially appear.

As in any city, some of the common public locations that offer free Wi-Fi in Vegas include ● **Clark County Libraries** ● **Fremont Street Experience** { _LV.NetFree } ● **Greyhound Bus Terminal** { GreyhoundTerminal FreeWIFI } ● **Henderson Libraries** ● **Las Vegas Convention Center** ● **McCarran International Airport** { McCarran WiFi } ● **RTC**

Buses { RTC Transit WiFi } • **RTC Transit Centers** { RTC Public WiFi } • **Monorail Station at Las Vegas Convention Center** •

As stated previously, with the advent of the resort fee, most casino properties now provide Wi-Fi as a resort fee amenity for hotel guests. But for non-guests, some properties also offer free Wi-Fi in public areas! Sign-in requirements vary by property and range from accepting terms & conditions to inserting a valid email address or players card number.

It is interesting to note that MGM Resorts International, the leader in reducing the amount of alcohol in a mixed drink and instituting parking fees, has also been the leader in offering free public Wi-Fi! Free Wi-Fi is available in public areas at: • **Aria** { AriaWi-Fi } • **Bellagio** { BellagioWiFi } • **Crystals** { CrystalsWi-Fi } • **Excalibur** { ExcaliburWiFi } • **Luxor** { LuxorWiFi } • **Mandalay Bay** { MandalayBayWiFi } **MGM Grand** { MGMGrandWiFi } • **Mirage** { MirageWiFi } • **Monte Carlo** { MonteCarloWiFi } • **New York-New York** { NYNYWiFi } • **The Park** { TheParkWiFi } • **Vdara** { VdaraWi-Fi } •

Caesars Entertainment offers free Wi-Fi in public areas at: • **Bally's** { BALLYS } • **Caesars Palace** { CAESARS } • **Flamingo** { FLAMINGO } • **Harrah's** { HARRAHS } • **The LINQ** { LINQ-HOTEL } • **Paris** { PARIS } • **Planet Hollywood** { PLANETHOLLYWOOD } •

Boyd Gaming has begun to offer free Wi-Fi in public areas at its properties. Sign-in is required with your B Connected Players Club card number. Currently available at: • **Orleans** { Boyd_Guest_WiFi } • **Gold Coast** { Boyd_Guest_WiFi } • **Suncoast** { Boyd_Guest_WiFi } •

Red Rock Resorts properties offer free Wi-Fi in public areas at • **Boulder Station** • **Fiesta Henderson** • **Fiesta Rancho** • **Green Valley Ranch** • **Palace Station** • **Red Rock Resort** • **Santa Fe Station** • **Sunset Station** • **Texas Station** • All properties = { STN-Guest } •

Other casino/hotel properties that offer free Wi-Fi in public areas include: • **Aliante** • **Cannery** { canneryguest } •

Eastside Cannery { eastsideguest) } ● Ellis Island Casino { ElFreeWiFi } ● JW Marriott Las Vegas Resort { JW_Marriott_LOBBY } ● SLS Hotel & Casino { SLS Guest }● The Plaza { _PLAZA } & Hash House-A-Go-Go in the Plaza { HashHouse } ● The Venetian & Palazzo { VenetianPalazzoWiFi } ● Westin { Westin-Lobby }● Wynn Las Vegas { Wynn Guest } ●

At resorts where free public area Wi-Fi is not offered, sometimes you can find free Wi-Fi being offered to customers by independent businesses within the resort. Some that come to mind include: ● The Coffee Bean & Tea Leaf (Green Valley Ranch, Palms, Palazzo, Planet Hollywood) ● Seattle's Best Coffee (South Point & Suncoast) ● Java Vegas Coffee (The Orleans & Suncoast) ● Pizza Place and Terrace Pointe Café (Wynn) ● (Individual Wi-Fi policies are subject to change)

As in any city, there are national chains that provide free Wi-Fi in the majority of their locations. These include: ● Starbucks (all non-hotel locations) ● Krispy Crème ● McDonalds ● Panera Bread ● Barnes & Noble ● Buffalo Wild Wings ● The Apple Store (Fashion Show Mall & Forum Shops @Caesars) ●

♠♥♣♦

Empowered with the wealth of information contained within this guide, there is no doubt you have begun planning your Vegas vacation. Keep in mind that there is so much to do and see in Vegas, that even a week-long visit would not be sufficient to enjoy all the city has to offer. The Strip and Downtown are like two separate adult amusement parks many miles distant, you cannot do either justice within a short visit.

Keep in mind when making your plans that time seems to fly by very quickly here in Vegas. Everything takes longer than you might expect. Distances can be deceiving, that short walk on the Strip taking in the sights and visiting different casinos, can be up to four miles long! Lines at show, attraction, buffet and restaurant venues normally move rather quickly, but there will be lines everywhere. And that planned short gaming session can easily turn into hours!

No matter how well you plan your days in Vegas, I guarantee that you'll never be able to complete your *To Do List*, take advantage of all the promotions, or use all your discount coupons and rewards in a single visit. But between your unused coupons, casino offers you'll soon be receiving, and the money this guide has helped you save, you should be well on your way to planning a return trip to fabulous Las Vegas!

♠♥♣♦

As has been stated previously, the gaming industry in Las Vegas is an extremely volatile market. Casinos, hotels and restaurants close and re-open. Casino resorts are built, acquired and sold. Policies, rates, hours and promotions constantly change and evolve. Typically published annually, travel guides can become outdated upon publication. For these reasons, if you have come across any inaccurate or outdated information within this guide, please share your discovery and corrections.

Likewise, should you discover something that the author has missed, or have tips and pointers of your own that might improve the Las Vegas experience for the next reader, please share them as well!

Finally, should this guide leave any unanswered questions concerning your visit to fabulous Las Vegas, please feel free to contact the author. Every effort will be made to provide an answer to your question! Please email all correspondence to: **frugallasvegas@yahoo.com**

For post publication updates, discoveries, news, reviews and information on current casino promotions, please visit, "like" and "share" the Facebook Page of this guide: **www.facebook.com/FrugalLasVegas**

♠♥♣♦

Made in the USA
San Bernardino, CA
02 September 2017